If my people, who are called by my name, will humble themselves and pray and seek my face and turn from their wicked ways, then will I hear from heaven and will forgive their sin and will heal their land.

2 Chronicles 7:14

AIDS is Real and It's in Our Church

Information about AIDS in Africa, how to prevent HIV infection, and encouragement towards a Christian response to the AIDS epidemic

C. Jean Garland

Mike Blyth

Africa Christian Textbooks

**TCNN, PMB 2020, Bukuru,
Plateau State, Nigeria**

OASIS INTERNATIONAL, LTD.

AIDS is Real and It's in Our Church

Revised Edition 2005

Copyright © C. Jean Garland 2003, 2004

ISBN: 1-59452-026-7

Most of the stories in this book are true, but to protect suffering individuals and families, all personal names and locations have been changed.

All illustrations by: Henry C. Ibegbunam

First published in 2003

**Africa Christian Textbooks
PMB 2020, Bukuru, Plateau State, Nigeria
Tel. 073-281055, 073-281546
Email: acts@hisen.org
http://www.africachristiantextbooks.com**

Copies of this book and others on AIDS, as well as theological books, are available from the ACTS branches listed under Resources, page 317.

Oasis International Limited exists to meet the unique needs of English speaking Africa, Asia, and the Caribbean. Oasis works to produce literature that is both relevant and affordable. For information contact Oasis International Ltd: info@oasisint.net.

Table of Contents

Dedication

This book is dedicated to all those who are infected and affected by HIV/AIDS in Africa, and who need to know the only true hope found in Jesus Christ who loves them and died for them.

Acknowledgements

God, our Father, who loves those with HIV/AIDS and gave me the ability to compile this book, deserves all the praise for this work.

Much of what I have learned about AIDS in Africa has been through my personal interactions and experiences. Since 1987, along with my husband and children, I have lived and worked in Nigeria, first in Akwa Ibom State and for the last 14 years in Plateau State. My training as a nurse and midwife helped me to supervise a primary health care clinic for several years. I have served God in a voluntary capacity with the Fellowship of Christian Students Aid for AIDS/Design for the Family programme, the ECWA AIDS Ministry, and the COCIN AIDS Awareness and Care Programme. I have also benefited from co-teaching a course at the Theological College of Northern Nigeria, where we used curriculum materials called, "Choosing Hope: The Christian Response to HIV/AIDS." Some valuable insights also came from helping write and teach a curriculum for Christian Religious Knowledge teachers and Islamic Studies teachers to use in primary and secondary schools in Nigeria. I have gained many insights at various conferences, both national and international, focusing on the issue of HIV/AIDS.

I am grateful to many people for their invaluable help in preparing the book.

I wish to acknowledge those living with HIV/AIDS who have shared their stories with me and the many groups and individuals all over Nigeria and elsewhere who have shared their experiences and have helped to give me a clearer insight into the challenges of HIV/AIDS in Africa.

My co-author and editor is Dr Mike Blyth, an SIM missionary paediatrician who has served at ECWA Evangel Hospital, Jos, for the past 13 years. His knowledge, faith, enthusiasm, and heart of compassion for those living with AIDS are reflected in the text.

My husband Dr Sid Garland has given me constant encouragement to commit to paper what I have learned. More than anyone, he inspired in me the confidence I needed to start and finish this book. Without him this project would never have been completed. He is my advisor, colleague, encourager and best friend. I thank God for him.

The Fellowship of Christian Students (a partner of Scripture Union, Africa) National Chairman, Mr Sam Udanyi and his wife Mrs Rhoda Udanyi invited me in 1997 to work with them in the Aid for AIDS/Design for the Family Programme of FCS. I have gained much wisdom from them and the other team members, Mr Paul Mershak and Mr Sunday Musa, as we have worked, travelled, and lived together tackling the AIDS issue.

Other advisors included Dr Musa Dankyau, Dr Silas Bot, Dr Elsbeth Young, Dr Janet Abaya, Rev. Luka Vandi, Rev. Bayo Oyebade, Mrs Margie Upson, Dr Danny McCain, and Miss Carmen McCain. I thank them all for their invaluable advice.

Mr Henry C. Ibegbunam, of "hi designs" (nig.) Jos, has used his God-given talents to draw all the illustrations. Henry has become our friend and has prayerfully shared the vision of what we desire this book to achieve. I thank God for his talents.

Jean Garland

May 2004

Introduction

"AIDS is Real and It's In Our Church." As the stories told in this book show, the weight of human suffering due to AIDS in Africa is daily increasing. Most of us realise by now that AIDS is real—we probably know people who have been affected by it, maybe someone close to us. But AIDS in the church—is it possible? In some countries the answer is already obvious as we have watched the brothers and sisters in our churches sicken and die. Elsewhere the plague has not reached such a height. Often we are not keen to admit that it is in the church. Often we think that the church should not become dirtied or spoiled by involving ourselves with those with AIDS. We see them as sinners paying for their sin. Meanwhile AIDS stalks our continent. It is killing our young people, yet a thick wall of silence surrounds the killer.

> Millions of our young people are already being lost to AIDS.

A proverb says, "The best time to plant a tree is twenty years ago. The next best time is now." Likewise, many years ago was the best time for all Christians in Africa to be addressing the issue of AIDS. Many are dying without God and without hope. However, the *next* best time to become involved is today.

The fire of AIDS raging all around the world gives Christians and the Church a unique opportunity to minister in Christ's name. It is a chance for us all to teach those around us how vital God's truth is for their lives. It is also a wonderful chance for us to demonstrate the love of Christ to the many who are in darkness and without any earthly hope. God's grace reaches to them. We must be the hands of Christ demonstrating that grace. When we are serving suffering people, we are serving him.

We pray that this book will be a tool in many hands to help equip us to face the tragedy of AIDS and to respond in a godly way. By God's grace and with the zeal and compassion of Christ, we can change the course of AIDS in Africa and bring many people to place their hope firmly in our Saviour, who died for sinners like us.

Whispers at the Burial: Isaac's Story

One wet, dark August day at a busy hospital, a thin and tired-looking young man slipped slowly behind the curtain of the room where Dr Chris was working. He slumped wearily onto a waiting chair. He refused to look the doctor straight in the eyes, but hung his head on his chest. Dr Chris was a good man with a kind face and searching eyes. He glanced at the patient's card and said,

"Good morning, Isaac. You are welcome. Tell me what the problem is, and I will see if I can help."

"Good morning," Isaac said. Then there was silence. The only noise was Isaac's shallow gasps and deep sighs. The doctor waited quietly for a short while. Again, he encouraged Isaac to talk.

Eventually, in a slow and weak voice, Isaac began to explain.

"I have such a painful mouth that I cannot eat. And my body is paining me, and I am feeling heat. At night, I wake up sweating. Now I have diarrhoea and a cough. I just feel so sick. For six months now I have been so sick."

Dr Chris put his hand on young Isaac's arm. It was thin like a stick. The flesh and muscle had nearly disappeared. Isaac's skin was hot, his eyes bright. With a resigned, tired tone, Isaac continued.

"I feel so alone. I do not know what to do. I am a third year law student. I am about to start my fourth year, but I cannot think about that. I am just so frightened."

From his experience, Dr Chris was sure Isaac had AIDS. Nevertheless, to confirm the diagnosis he needed to test Isaac's blood. He gently explained to Isaac that he might have AIDS, and that a blood test was required. Isaac was troubled but agreed to have the test. Later that day the result came back from the laboratory, showing that he did have HIV.

Isaac is only one young man out of the millions who are dying from AIDS in Africa and worldwide. The nightmare of AIDS that Isaac faced is real to many suffering young people in Africa. Yet some Africans are still looking the other way. They do not want to know, or do not want to admit that they know, what is happening.

Isaac only lived for five weeks after that first visit to the hospital. He refused to tell his family he had AIDS. He said that they would reject him. The family was sure that someone had put a curse on their son, and even when Isaac died, no one mentioned AIDS. His family wondered and worried, but hid their fear and refused to face the facts. There were many whispers at Isaac's burial.[1]

Discussion Questions

1. Discuss what you think were the reasons that Isaac's family were not able to talk about the true cause of their son's death. Why do you think that they blamed his death on witchcraft?

2. What do you think may have been the reasons that Isaac was not able to talk to his parents about his illness?

---

[1] Based on a true story

Chapter One
What Are HIV and AIDS?

Human Immunodeficiency Virus (HIV)

Viruses cause many different illnesses, such as the common cold (catarrh), measles, hepatitis A, B and C, chickenpox, polio, and rabies. The *human immunodeficiency virus* (HIV) that causes AIDS is a small germ that is too small to see with an ordinary microscope. It is so small that there could be 230,000 at the point of a pen or on a full stop at the end of a sentence.[2] It only takes a few of these viruses to enter your body for you to become infected and later develop the condition we call AIDS. AIDS is not a disease caused by witchcraft, or directly from God, or from bad water, or from mosquitoes, but one caused by a virus.

---

[2] Fellowship of Christian Students, *Towards an AIDS Free Generation.*

HIV[3] belongs to a group of viruses called *retroviruses*. There are several types (varieties) of HIV. There are many types of the virus found in different areas of the world, especially in different areas of Africa. If you are infected with any type of HIV, and you are not treated with antiretroviral drugs, you will almost certainly develop AIDS and die within two to fourteen years. If you get good medical care and take antiretroviral drugs properly, you may live longer but will likely die of AIDS in the end.

HUMAN: The virus is only found in humans. It is not found in animals or insects.

IMMUNODEFICIENCY: The virus reduces the defence power of the *immune* system. The immune system has the job of protecting the body from all kinds of infections and invaders. It destroys germs that enter the body. The next section explains this in more detail.

VIRUS: A virus is a germ too small to see with a regular light microscope. People must use powerful electron microscopes to see HIV. Viruses are the smallest of all micro-organisms (germs), hundreds of times smaller than a bacteria or malaria parasite.

What is the immune system?

The immune system is the body's Ministry of Defence. Germs are all around us, some of them getting into our bodies from the day we are born. Most are harmless but some can make us sick. Our immune system protects us from those germs. The immune system keeps us from getting very sick. To understand our immune system we can compare its job to what a country's

---

[3] Strictly speaking, we are referring to HIV–1. There is a very similar virus, HIV–2, which often does not lead as quickly to AIDS. HIV–2, which used to be somewhat common in West Africa, appears to be disappearing at the same time that HIV–1 is on the rise.

armed forces do to protect it. If the defences (military) are weak or not working, then enemies can invade our country.

For example, the *white blood cells* in our blood are part of the immune system. They are soldiers on the attack against germs that enter our bodies. HIV kills many of those white blood cells so that they can no longer protect the body as they should.

When the immune system is working well, we can see evidence of that. For example, when a person has a throat infection, the *lymph nodes* in his neck may become swollen and tender, obvious to the person himself and to the doctor. The swollen lymph nodes show that the immune system is fighting the throat infection.

HIV attacks the body's defences

HIV attacks the white blood cells, especially ones called *CD4 cells (or T helper cells)*. It attaches to the cell and then enters it. The virus multiplies by using the cell's own production "factories" to make copies of itself. HIV eventually kills the CD4 cells.

The CD4 cells are like the coordinators of the immune system. They gather information and pass it to the rest of the immune system. They are the eyes and ears, the radar and telephone, of the body's army.

We can compare the CD4 cells to the Ministry of Information. They both analyse and pass along important messages. Try to imagine what would happen to a country if, after the armed forces were weakened, the Ministry of Information was also destroyed. The country would be in chaos. Important information would not be passed on.

The *CD4 count* is a measure of how many CD4 cells are working in the body. A healthy person's CD4 count is between

650 and 1250.[4] In a person infected with HIV, when the CD4 count drops below 200 and certain germs invade the body, the person is said to have AIDS. Doctors do not usually start antiretroviral drug therapy[5] until the patient's CD4 count drops to around 350 or less.

When the CD4 cells are destroyed, the whole immune system does not work in harmony. The body's protection against infection is gradually worn away. This allows many different infections to enter the body and destroy it.

What is AIDS?

Local names for AIDS

The word "AIDS" causes confusion in the minds of some people. Because the word sounds like the number eight, people in some areas call it "eight." In some places, it is known as 7+1, 10-2, 4+4, 6+2, 3+5 and 9-1! Some people call it "positive disease," "monkey disease," "modern disease," "disease of eight," "tomorrow is too far," "dig your own grave," and "skinny disease" or "slim disease." In Tanzania AIDS is called "walking corpse" and in Zambia it is referred to as "keys to the mortuary."

In truth, AIDS is a group of signs and symptoms that develop towards the end of the life of a person infected with HIV.[6]

The acronym A-I-D-S is for the following words.

---

[4] That is, between 650 and 1250 cells per cubic millimetre.

[5] "Antiretroviral drugs" are drugs that fight HIV. Remember that HIV is a type of virus called a *retrovirus*. These drugs are still very costly and are not easily available in some African countries. See Chapter Twelve.

[6] In medical language, signs are things that can be seen or found by a doctor and symptoms are things that a person complains that he/she is feeling or experiencing. For example, skin rashes are a sign because anyone can see them. Itching is a symptom, something the patient complains of.

ACQUIRED: That is, it is a disease that people get or catch, not one they are born with.[7] The virus is passed from person to person, including often from mother to baby. An infected person gets or *acquires* the virus that causes AIDS from someone else who already has the virus.

IMMUNE: HIV attacks the immune system. The word "immune" speaks of protection or defence.

DEFICIENCY: There is a deficient, inadequate, or "less-than-needed" response to all diseases by the immune system.

SYNDROME: Any syndrome is just a group of signs and symptoms. When a person has AIDS, there is a group of signs and symptoms that point to that fact. Later we will discuss these signs and symptoms of AIDS (see page 30).

What are the stages leading to AIDS?

Most diseases that are spread through sex are followed by obvious signs that appear within a few days of the infection, such as a discharge from the private parts or an ulcer on the private parts. This is not so with HIV infection.

> Nine out of 10 people infected with the HIV virus do not know that they have it

Nine out of ten people infected with HIV are unaware that they have it. Most only learn of their infection when they start to become sick with AIDS-related illnesses. Those illnesses may make the doctor think of HIV, so that he orders a blood test, showing HIV infection. But the person has usually been infected with HIV for years.

---

[7] Babies can be born with the virus, but they are not born with AIDS.

1. Window period

At the beginning of the HIV infection, a person may have no symptoms at all. Some people may have a slight fever and symptoms similar to malaria a few days after the virus enters their body, but those symptoms soon disappear. *Most people do not notice any illness or symptoms around the time of infection.*

The HIV test may remain negative for three months or, rarely, even six months after the initial infection. This is because there are not yet enough antibodies to cause the test to read positive (see page 43). The time before the blood test becomes positive is called the "window period." The window period is a very dangerous time for others because the infected person's HIV test result will be negative, but he or she can infect others through sex or through blood transfusion. The person has a large amount of HIV in the blood during this time—50,000 or more virus particles in a single drop. The window period is a time of especially great risk to those receiving blood transfusions, as the donated blood will appear free from HIV, but will be deadly to the person who receives it.

2. Symptom-free period

We say the window period has ended when someone's HIV test result becomes positive. Although the *test* is now positive, the person will notice nothing new and will never suspect that they have HIV. Without testing the blood, even a doctor could not detect the infection. From the time of infection through the next 2–10 years, someone with HIV has no symptoms but *can* transmit HIV to others. This is the symptom-free (*asymptomatic*) period. The person will look healthy and will be active. Many people believe that they will not contract HIV if they have sexual contact only with healthy looking individuals. They are sadly

> AIDS no dey show for face

mistaken. You cannot tell who is living with HIV by looking at them. As the slogan says, "AIDS no dey show for face."

3. Symptomatic period

In time, usually after several years, the person living with HIV starts to develop symptoms such as tiredness, fever, dysentery, cough, enlarged lymph nodes ("glands"), weight loss, skin rashes and yeast infections of the mouth or, in women, of the genitals. This means that he or she has entered the *symptomatic period*. The person may start attending the clinic or hospital often, with malaria or other fevers, cough, rashes, and diarrhoea.

Many *opportunistic* illnesses come into the body at this time. The healthy body, without HIV, can fight off these diseases without medicines. But when the body's defences are weak, these diseases take advantage of the *opportunity* to come into the body and cause illness. That is why doctors call these diseases "opportunistic diseases." Many people with HIV infection develop skin problems of some kind. Chronic diarrhoea and *thrush* (a whitish rash in the mouth) are two examples of opportunistic infections. People in the symptomatic stage may also have continuing or repeated fevers.

Tuberculosis (TB) is another disease that is common in people with a weakened immune system. TB can also infect people with normal immune systems, but it is more likely to cause disease in people when HIV has weakened their defences. Medicine for tuberculosis will cure the disease in most people without HIV and those with HIV who have not reached the stage of AIDS. People with AIDS, though, may continue to struggle with TB despite treatment.

Let us look more closely at some of the common signs and symptoms of HIV at this stage:

- *Yeast infections.* Thrush is a yeast infection of the mouth. This is a white, milky coating inside the person's mouth, throat, or both. It can be quite painful. The same yeast can cause a painful, itching infection of the female genitals. Yeast infections are found in many people with HIV/AIDS. They are also common in healthy babies below six months of age and sometimes in people who have recently taken antibiotic medicines for some time. Female genital yeast infection can also occur in healthy women without HIV.

- *Persistent cough.* Tuberculosis or other chest infection often causes this.

- *Mild body weakness.* Of course, many illnesses can cause weakness. By itself it is not a sign of HIV. But the person with HIV may begin to lose energy and to feel tired and unwell much of the time.

- *Continuing fevers and night sweats.* Tuberculosis by itself can also cause these night sweats, as can some other illnesses.

- *Little desire to eat.* Doubtless, some of the other results of AIDS such as mouth sores contribute to loss of appetite in people with AIDS. Of course, there are many causes of loss of appetite including other illnesses, worry, sadness, weakness, and lack of tasty food.

- *Persistent skin rashes.* These rashes may cover large areas of the body and are often itchy. The skin may even peel off much of the body causing the person's appearance to change.

- *Herpes infection.* The herpes virus causes "cold sores" around the mouth or in the genital area. Healthy people can also get the sores, but they usually fight them off after some days. The sores often return even in healthy people, but more often and for a longer time in those infected with HIV.

- *Shingles.* This is a viral infection with painful rashes and sometimes open sores, usually on one side of the body. In Africa, shingles occur in about ten percent of those with AIDS.
- *Swollen* lymph *nodes ("glands")* found especially under the arms and in the groin area, but also in the neck. There are many other causes of such swellings.[8]

The symptomatic period can last for several years before the last stage, AIDS, begins. The length of time before AIDS depends partly on whether the person has the money to buy needed drugs, especially antibiotics to treat infections, is eating well and is living in a healthy way. There is no clear dividing line between the symptomatic period and the last period, which is called AIDS. It is common for people to live six to eight years from the time of infection until reaching the stage of AIDS, but no one can predict the length of time for a given person.

4. AIDS

You will remember we said that AIDS is a group of signs and symptoms. Until this stage, the person was an HIV carrier. The HIV test was positive but the symptoms were irregular as the opportunistic diseases came and went. Now, at the end stage, problems and illnesses begin increasing. The person's health worsens to the point of continuous illness, and he or she is said to have AIDS. The person is an AIDS patient. The period of

---

[8] WHO Case Definitions for AIDS Surveillance in Adults and Adolescents. *Weekly Epidemiological Record* 69(37):273-5, 1994, and 1993 Revised Classification System for HIV Infection and Expanded Surveillance Case Definition for AIDS among Adolescents and Adults. *MMWR Recomm Rep 41(RR-17)*:1-19, 1992.

AIDS is the short time (usually less than a year without antiretroviral treatment) before death.

As we said, there is no clear dividing line between the symptomatic period and AIDS. Some signs and symptoms of AIDS may appear before AIDS fully develops. With treatment, they may improve or disappear for some time only to return later.

Signs of AIDS

AIDS can appear in many forms. Even a trained doctor may not be able to say whether someone has AIDS simply by examining him or her. Illnesses like tuberculosis and cancer can appear identical to AIDS. This is why a blood test is needed in order to say whether a person has HIV/AIDS. Certain signs, though, show that the HIV-infected person has probably reached the stage of AIDS. These include

- Persistent *fever* lasting more than one month
- *Excessive weight loss,* losing ten percent of body weight
- *Persistent diarrhoea* lasting more than one month
- *Severe body weakness,* having to stay in bed most of the time

Some illnesses of AIDS are simply more severe forms of those in the earlier symptomatic period. For example, thrush may spread from the mouth down into the oesophagus (where food passes from the mouth to the stomach) or trachea (breathing tube). Likewise, tuberculosis may spread from the lungs into many other areas of the body. Until this stage, the body has been able to fight infections somewhat, but now the defences are crumbling and the infections begin to win.

Some other signs of AIDS are cancers like Kaposi's sarcoma, which may first show on the legs. Others are unusual illnesses like a chest infection called *Pneumocystis carinii* pneumonia

(PCP) and cytomegalovirus (CMV). CMV affects the brain, eyes, and other organs, and can lead to blindness and other neurological problems. Infections or cancer of the brain may lead to loss of ability to move, walk, or talk properly, or to other neurological problems.

It is important to realise that none of these problems is a sure sign of AIDS. A doctor or health worker should make the diagnosis after considering the whole picture. Whenever possible, a laboratory test should be done to confirm or reject the diagnosis of HIV. We should *never* start rumours that someone has AIDS. Many people with severe weight loss do not have AIDS. Many people with skin problems, TB and cancers do not have AIDS. Therefore, we should never jump to conclusions or start rumours. AIDS is a private matter.

Laboratory Tests: Towards the end of life the antibody tests for HIV have been known in some cases to become negative as the immune system can no longer produce antibodies even to the virus itself. As has been mentioned, in some areas a test is available to measure the CD4 count in a person's blood. If the CD4 count is below 200, the person is said to now have AIDS.

The person with AIDS is unlikely to be very active sexually as he or she is too ill. However, those who *are* having sexual activity are extremely infectious to others. Their viral load is quite high and the CD4 count is quite low. After reaching this stage, without the help of antiretroviral drugs, the person will usually die within a year or two. Medicines to treat the opportunistic diseases are of little help at this stage and the illnesses become continuous. The immune system is destroyed. Often AIDS is not listed as the cause of death on the death certificate, but rather one of the illnesses that brought death, like tuberculosis, diarrhoea, typhoid or even malaria.

Factors influencing the progression to AIDS

Health before infection

If the person is in good health before being infected with HIV, then the virus will be slower to destroy the body's immune system and the person will be likely to live longer.

Treatment and prevention of opportunistic infections

Proper treatment of any infections that do enter the body will help the HIV-infected person to remain healthier and live longer. Many people do not have enough money for good treatment even though they want to care for themselves properly. The family and the church can help practically with finances for treatment. Sometimes people may not seek treatment because they are discouraged, depressed or embarrassed. Family and church members can encourage them and help them get the care they need. This kind of assistance and encouragement will help people with HIV live longer, healthier lives.

When the immune system is weakened, doctors often prescribe a daily antibiotic to prevent certain infections. For example, the inexpensive drug co-trimoxazole[9] taken once daily helps prevent some opportunistic infections. Doctors prescribe it for many patients with HIV. This simple preventive measure can add from two to three years to the person's life.

Diet and vitamins

Good nutrition clearly improves the health of HIV-infected people. They are likely to stay healthier longer by eating healthy foods. This means that along with the starch found in the staple

---

[9] Septrin or Bactrim

foods like maize, guinea corn, cassava, yam, rice, semovita, millet or potato, they need to eat foods containing proteins, minerals, and vitamins. Protein is best found in meat, fish, chicken, eggs, beans, soya beans, lentils, dark greens, and groundnuts. Fresh fruits and vegetables (such as carrots, dark greens, and tomatoes) are rich in some vitamins, special parts of food that keep the body working well. Soft fruits like papaya, bananas or mangoes help digestion. *Variety* is the key! People who eat a good variety of these foods are likely to stay healthier longer than those with a poor diet containing mainly starch. Drinking plenty of pure water is also important.

The body needs *vitamins* or it will become weak and sick. Because people with HIV often do not eat well, they may not get the vitamins they need. For this reason, they should take multi-vitamin tablets or syrup. Multi-vitamins are safe, they are not costly, and they will help people remain with HIV remain healthy. You can find them in most pharmacies. Be sure that they are fresh and not past the expiration date.

Two infected persons can shorten each other's lives

There is some evidence that a couple who are both HIV-infected might shorten their lives if they continue to have sexual intercourse with each other. This is because they could infect each other with different varieties of the virus.[10] Some of these different varieties could destroy more CD4 cells or be more resistant to treatment. If a couple are both infected, it is best that they regularly and consistently use condoms to help avoid pregnancy and re-exposure to HIV.

---

[10] A person who is infected with one type (strain or "clade") of HIV can still become infected with second type. This is called "super-infection" (where "super" means "on top of" and not extra powerful). New varieties are being produced every day in infected people. So even if two people began with the same variety, one could develop a "worse" variety and pass it to the other.

Personal care

Personal hygiene is important for people living with HIV/AIDS. They need to wash well morning and evening, wash their hands well after going to the toilet, avoid smoking and alcohol, and take plenty of rest. They should stay away from people with infectious diseases like tuberculosis, chickenpox or measles. At the same time, it is good for their spirits and minds if they stay active and busy, rather than become depressed sitting around waiting for the end of their lives.

Discussion Questions

1. Do you think it is important for Christians to look at HIV/AIDS as a health issue rather than a moral issue only? Why or why not?

2. Are there names for AIDS in your local language? Why do you think many of the names give a negative picture of AIDS?

3. Discuss what your local church and community can do to educate others that HIV infection does not show on the outside of the body.

4. How do you think we can help each other, especially in our local church, to make right choices today that will lead to good results years later, rather than wrong choices today that will bring pain and death years later?

I had dreams for my family ...

"My husband was the first man I allowed to touch me."

Sarah sat slouched in the chair, looking at the floor, not yet having the confidence to raise her eyes to meet mine.

"Tell me your story, Sarah. What has happened to you? Just explain to me what has happened. I want to know."

"I was 26 when I wedded and my husband was 36. We were from the same village. I am a Catholic and I kept myself for my husband, just as the church teaches. My husband was the first man I allowed to touch me.

"In 1996, we had the traditional wedding and then the church wedding shortly afterwards. Not long after we wedded, my husband became sick. We went to hospital, and they said that he had TB. I was tested and I also had TB. We both took the treatment.

"In 1997, I fell pregnant and our little girl was born. But she was always sick and so, so small. I have never seen a baby so small before. She refused to grow.

"In 1998, my husband became very sick and died. I did not know then what made him so sick or caused him to die. One month later, my little girl also died. Again, I did not know what happened that made her so sick and caused her to die.

"I went back to live with my family and since then have helped my senior brother in his shop. I have never been with another man, only my husband."

"I am so sorry, Sarah. That must have been very difficult for you," I said.

"Yes," she said, raising her eyes for the first time. "It was a terrible time."

"This year, 2002, I started to get itchy rashes all over my body. I am not able to sleep at night.. And everyone asks me what is causing the rash."

Sarah pulled up her skirt to show me the dark scars where open sores had been. She was wearing a long skirt and long sleeves to hide her suffering.

"Then I went to the hospital. The doctor took an HIV test and when I went back for the result, he told me I had HIV infection. Since then I have been using aloe vera to help the rashes.

"I was so shocked. I went home and cried on my bed for about two weeks. I knew then, for the first time, that my husband and baby must have died from AIDS and that I too will die from AIDS."

Sarah looked up at me. She continued, "I had dreams for my family. All I wanted was to have a good husband and a happy home and children. That is why I kept myself only for my husband."

"Those were good dreams to have, Sarah. Most girls have those dreams for a happy family life."

She continued, "My family did not know what was wrong with me. I just wanted to die. I could not eat. Then I remembered a man and his wife who were kind and caring when my husband died. I decided to go and tell them. The next day I did just that. They listened to me and prayed with me and sent me to talk to an AIDS counsellor at the hospital. After I talked to her, I got the courage to tell my family. In fact, the night I talked to her, I called my family together. My elderly father and my brother and the younger ones—I told them all that I had HIV.

"They were so angry. They were not angry with me, but with my dead husband for bringing such suffering to our family. They said that they would try to take care of me. I hope that I can get the money to get the anti-AIDS drugs that I have read about.

"Now that I have been able to tell some people about having HIV, I feel better. If only I could get help to ease this rash."

"Sarah, we will see what we can do to help you ease the rash. And we will keep praying that God will help you to live with HIV. Thank you for telling me your story."

Sarah smiled for the first time since she came to see me. Having someone to listen to her story seemed to help her.

As Sarah left, I thought of the way her tragedy is being repeated again and again all over Africa. It is a fact that many if not most African women living with HIV/AIDS were infected by their husbands. Do these men realise the measure of suffering that their behaviour is bringing to their families? I doubt it.

I pray, "Dear God, please cause our African men today to turn to you in repentance and faith, and help them to make a difference to the story of AIDS in Africa."[11]

---

[11] A true story from Nigeria

Chapter Two
What is an HIV Test and
Where Can I Get One?

Tests for HIV are becoming more and more available across Africa, especially in the cities and towns. HIV testing is important in the war against HIV/AIDS. These tests will detect the infection soon after a person becomes infected and long before illness appears.[12] Why would someone want to know that they are infected? In the past, many people have *not* wanted to know because they felt that there was nothing to be done. Now, however, we know that people who learn early that they are infected can take action to live healthier, longer lives. With antiretroviral drugs, they might even have a normal lifespan. Knowing that they are infected can help them to protect the people they love from becoming infected also. However, all this

---

[12] I often hear people say that they have gone for an "AIDS test." Actually, what they probably mean is an "HIV test." There is no such thing as an AIDS test. AIDS is a group of problems and illnesses that occur after the body's defence system has been destroyed by HIV. For example, weight loss and chronic diarrhoea are two of the problems. AIDS is a diagnosis that a doctor makes when he sees a person showing these signs and symptoms.

depends on *knowing* that one is infected, and that is the purpose of testing.

Reasons people choose to be tested for HIV

People may choose get an HIV test for many reasons. Everyone has their own reasons. Some common reasons are:

- signs and symptoms that cause them to worry that they are infected;
- worry that their sexual partners are infected;
- wanting to be tested before marriage;
- planning to have a baby;
- concern after the husband or wife has died of unknown causes
- knowing that they might have been exposed in the past through blood exposure or sex.

In addition, all blood prepared for transfusion to another person *must* be tested for HIV.

If you decide that you would like to have an HIV test, go only to a clinic or VCT centre that gives counselling before and after testing. Why? It is best to have some mental preparation before receiving the result. When you receive the result you should also have someone talk with you about its meaning and importance. Go to a clinic or centre where you know that there are skilled laboratory technicians, and where you know that your test result will be kept confidential. (Chapter Fourteen discusses pre- and post-test counselling.)

What is an HIV carrier?

For most of the years after infection by HIV, the person is known as an *HIV carrier*. Just as a woman carries bananas in the market, and stops and gives some to various people as she passes by, so the person with HIV in his or her blood carries the virus around and can pass it on to others. However, unlike the woman with the bananas, often the person himself and those around him are unaware that the virus is present as there are no symptoms to show its effects.

To have an HIV test or not is your own decision

Whether or not to have an HIV test is something that an individual must choose of his or her own free will. A church or employer cannot force someone to have an HIV test. They can suggest a test for the person's own good. A church can choose not to marry people who refuse the test, but they cannot force someone to be tested. According to the International Guidelines on HIV/AIDS and Human Rights, no employer has the right to require his or her employees to have an HIV test. The declaration states, "Everyone should have access to employment without any preconditions except the necessary occupational qualifications. This right is violated when an applicant or employee is required to undergo mandatory testing for HIV and is refused employment or dismissed or refused access to employee benefits on the grounds of a positive result." [13]

Unfortunately, African churches have often required HIV testing before employing workers. Sometimes they have required testing in order for workers to continue in their jobs. Moreover, if the result is positive, the person tested is then dismissed from employment. It is clear that these churches are using the test to "find out" those who are infected and not to counsel and help them. A positive test is often seen as an indication of sin, and yet no one can know where the virus came from. Even if it did come by a sinful act, that act may have happened many years previously, perhaps when the person did not know the Saviour. Now he or she is following Christ and is active in his service.

What does an HIV test show?

The common tests for HIV show *antibodies* to the virus, not the virus itself. The virus itself is too small to be seen under most microscopes.

Antibodies are substances produced by white blood cells. Their job is to help destroy specific germs. White blood cells make antibodies only to the kinds of germs that have already invaded the body. The antibodies are evidence of the body's reaction against an infection. Therefore, a person has HIV antibodies only if he or she has already been infected with HIV.[14] The usual tests for HIV detect these antibodies in the blood. When antibodies are found, the person is said to be HIV positive. Sometimes the word *seropositive* or *reactive* is used. Sometimes

---

[13] Office of the High Commissioner for Human Rights (OHCHR)/UNAIDS: HIV/AIDS and Human Rights: International Guidelines (New York and Geneva, 1998).

[14] Babies, however, can receive antibodies before birth from their mothers, even when they are not infected.

the laboratory form will say that the person has retroviral disease (RVD). If no antibodies to HIV are found, the person is said to be HIV negative or *seronegative or non-reactive.*

The body does not produce antibodies immediately after HIV infection. Large numbers of virus are in the blood and can pass to other people, but the antibodies are not yet present. The antibody tests cannot detect them until about one to three months, and in rare cases six months, after the infection. This means that for the first weeks or months after infection by HIV, the blood test will be negative even though the person is infected and *can pass the virus to other people.* This time is known as the "window period." During the window period, the person is infected and can pass the virus to others, but the HIV test does not yet show the infection.

An *antigen* test, which detects the virus itself rather than the antibodies, becomes positive a few days after the virus enters the body. These tests are not yet easily available in Africa. They detect the virus earlier, so that the window period is much shorter. This reduces the time of uncertain diagnosis.

Types of HIV tests

The most readily available HIV tests are blood tests.[15] The most common of these in Africa are the rapid tests and the ELISA test.[16] Rapid tests are easy for laboratories to use and give results in less than an hour. ELISA tests are similar but somewhat slower. If a person tests positive with one of these, the doctor may recommend confirming the result using another, different test. If the person already has many signs and symptoms of AIDS, the doctor may conclude from the rapid test

---

[15] There are also HIV antibody tests that can be done using saliva or urine, but these are generally not available in most parts of Africa. However, they may be more available soon.

[16] ELISA stands for enzyme linked immuno-sorbent assay.

or ELISA alone that the person is HIV positive. Another antibody test that is used in some laboratories is the *western blot*.

After the window period, rapid tests and ELISA are almost always positive in a patient infected with HIV. However, if the test is negative but the health worker suspects HIV because of the patient's signs and symptoms, he or she may order repeated tests to look for a positive result.

Testing for HIV infection in young babies

It is difficult to confirm HIV infection in young babies who may have been infected by their mothers. The usual blood tests cannot show with certainty that the baby has HIV, only that the mother has it. Why is this?

A baby is born with an immature and inexperienced immune system. This defence system will become mature and gain experience during the first year of a baby's life. How is the baby protected from diseases in the first months of life? Partly by the *mother's* antibodies.

Before birth, the mother's antibodies cross from the mother into the baby's blood across the placenta (after-birth). The mother also gives her baby antibodies through her breast milk. In the first few days after birth, the first breast milk, called *colostrum*, is particularly rich in these valuable, protective antibodies.

Antibodies against HIV join the other antibodies that pass to the baby from the infected mother. If the baby of an HIV-infected mother has a test for HIV antibodies in the early months of life, the baby will *always* test positive for HIV antibodies. The reason is not that the baby is infected, but that the baby is carrying the antibodies of the mother's infection.

Even if the baby is not infected, the HIV blood test will remain positive for up to 18 months after the birth. The antibodies slowly leave the blood. After about 18 months the blood test will be negative if the antibodies were only from the mother. If the baby does have HIV infection, the blood test will *remain* positive because the baby starts to produce its own antibodies to HIV.

Some well-meaning medical workers who do not understand this issue have tested babies born to HIV positive mothers. Of course, as you now know, the babies will all be HIV positive. The workers may have abandoned giving some babies the usual good medical care, thinking that their lives will be short, and that they are not worth caring for. Instead, they should have cared for these babies as well as any other, knowing that it is only after about one-and-a-half years of life that they can be sure of the babies' HIV status. Even if the babies *are* infected, we still need to care for them as valuable individuals created by God and worthy of our love.

Some more advanced laboratories may be able to test a baby's blood for the presence of the HIV virus itself, rather than antibodies. This can allow doctors to know by the age of six months whether or not the baby is infected.

Voluntary Counselling and Testing (VCT) Centres

There are many VCT centres, sometimes called VTC centres, in most African countries.

A concerned individual can come off the street and ask for an HIV test. A trained counsellor will talk with him or her before and after the test. Pre-test counselling is valuable to help clients understand and prepare for the test results. Post-test counselling is also important for explaining the results and for giving

guidelines for healthy living. The counsellors must keep in confidence all information the person gives.

Some people need time, after the first counselling session, before they are ready to return for testing. A good counsellor will help people think about the advantages and disadvantages of knowing their status. Whether or not to be tested is a personal decision. (See Chapter Fourteen on Pastoral Counselling.)

For those who are found to be HIV-infected, trained counsellors will give hope and support towards making life as worthwhile and healthy as possible. The infected person can also learn how not to infect others. Counsellors will help non-infected people learn how to protect themselves from becoming infected.

Voluntary testing and counselling is available at many government and private hospitals and health centres. Some church-operated clinics also offer the service. Many more VCT centres need to be established all over Africa so that those who wish to know their HIV status can be tested and counselled. Besides its benefits for the individual, VCT is a vital part of the effort to bring HIV/AIDS into the open and to reduce stigma and discrimination.[17]

It is really only after someone is tested for HIV that they can genuinely encourage others to go for an HIV test. If you are a pastor or church leader and you want your members to be tested, you must first go for your own HIV test.

Advantages of being tested

There are many advantages to being tested for HIV.

If you are found to be infected:

- You can receive early treatment and perhaps live longer.
- You can make decisions to take good care of yourself.
- You can develop a good emotional support group around you in the early stages of the disease.
- Knowing that three out of ten babies born to infected mothers will become infected (without the help of antiretroviral drugs), you can make a decision whether or not to become pregnant. If you do become pregnant, you will be able to take action to try to prevent passing HIV to your baby.
- You can inform your spouse or partner that you have HIV.
- You can abstain from sex so as not to infect others.
- You can avoid sharing any items that come in contact with blood.
- You will decide not to give blood to others.

---

[17] The "stigma" of HIV means that people with HIV are seen as being different, bad, unclean, sinners, or in other ways not good. "Discrimination" means that people are treated unequally. For example, a person may lose his job because he has HIV.

If you are found not to be infected, you will be relieved to know the result and will want to live in a way that keeps you HIV negative.

Medical personnel, even doctors, need to be educated to refer inquirers to counsellors for help. Sometimes health workers and doctors simply dismiss their patients who are living with HIV/AIDS, without referring them to someone who can help them. The attitude of many medical workers remains one of hopelessness and abandonment, rather than on-going support and help.

Pre-marital testing

Voluntary testing is especially important for all couples before marriage. This *pre-marital* testing is practised widely in many African countries. No one can force couples to be tested, but we can certainly encourage them to do so by explaining the reasons for testing.

Many religious leaders feel that it is wrong to perform a marriage ceremony joining an infected person to an uninfected person. They know the deadly disease will probably be passed on from one partner to the other. Some of the couple's children will likely be infected also. Even ones who are not infected will probably become orphans.[18]

These religious leaders feel that if they join a couple in marriage when one or both partners are infected and expect to have children, it is as if the leader is approving of a marriage that might multiply death and suffering rather than blessing. Such decisions are difficult and the pastor and church leadership should consider them carefully and prayerfully.

---

[18] Pre-marital testing and counselling are discussed further in Chapter Fourteen.

Pastors and other religious leaders may sometimes decide to marry a couple knowing that one or both are infected by HIV. In this case they must certainly help the couple clearly understand all of the facts about AIDS. Before deciding to marry, the couple must know all the facts, including the risks to themselves and any future children.

Discussion Questions

1. If your friend is afraid that he or she may have HIV infection, what advice would you give him or her? Why would you give this advice?

2. Discuss the reasons why many people are fearful of having an HIV test.

3. Discuss what the negative effects on your community would be if the government introduced compulsory HIV testing for all adults.

4. Some African local churches are paying for their members to be tested for HIV, not with the purpose of disciplining them, but to help everyone know their status, to make AIDS more open, and thus to prevent further infections. Do you think this idea would work in your country and in your church? What advantages and disadvantages would such a plan have?

If only I had said "NO" to Uncle! Naomi's story

Naomi was 12 years old and lived with her parents and her five younger brothers and sisters in a small village. Naomi was the oldest child in her family. Her father was away from home most of the time because he drove a big lorry for a company that sold cement all over Uganda. Her mother was away from home most of the day, too. She went to the market to sell yams and soup vegetables. Naomi was often at home on her own, caring for her brothers and sisters. She had to do most of the cooking, sweeping and even bathing the younger ones. She went to school in the mornings, but in the afternoons she farmed and worked in the compound.

Naomi had an uncle who often came to the house. She would give him a drink of water from the well, and they would sit and talk. There was no one else to listen. The younger ones just played. Uncle was kind and seemed to listen to her. He would often tell her how beautiful she was and tease her about how one day she would have a fine husband. Uncle's wife had died earlier that year and he seemed so sad at times. Mother and Father were not there and often Naomi was lonely. She enjoyed having Uncle to listen.

One day, Uncle came to the compound. He sat inside the hut and was very quiet. Naomi sat opposite him. Uncle was looking at her in a funny, disturbing way. Naomi wondered why he was looking at her like that. Then Uncle told Naomi to come and sit beside him. She did as she was told, and Uncle put his arm around her shoulders. He started to say nice things to her in a soft, sweet voice. He told her that she was a wonderful girl. He told her that she was beautiful and clever and that he loved her very much.

No one had ever told Naomi that she was loved. She felt warm inside to know that this could be true. Then Uncle shocked her. He said that they could have a little secret together that no one else would know. If Naomi would let him have sex with her, he would pay her school fees and make sure that she could go to the big secondary school in the town.

Naomi was scared inside. She did not know much about sex. No one had ever told her. She had heard her friends laugh about sex. She did love Uncle and wanted to please him. She had been taught to do what she was told, especially for the senior members of the family. Moreover, she did want to go to the big secondary school in the town. She did not know how to say "no" to Uncle.

After it was over, Naomi was crying. He had hurt her. She felt dirty and ashamed of what she had done. She did not feel proud to have Uncle "love" her. Uncle made her promise to keep their secret. He said if she told anyone there would be no school fees. There was no one whom she could tell what had happened. Indeed, Uncle came back to Naomi many more times and every time Naomi said "yes" to his demands.

Naomi did go to the big secondary school in the town. She did very well. She made many good friends. She did not think much about what she had done with Uncle until one day she heard that he was quite sick. Her mother and father talked in low voices about how Uncle had AIDS. They even said that Auntie had died from AIDS and that Uncle would soon die. What was AIDS? Naomi did not know much but she did know that AIDS was spread by sex. Fear gripped her heart. However, she pushed it away and tried not to think about it.

It was the year Naomi was to move into senior secondary school that she became sick. She always seemed to have fever and diarrhoea. Mother and Father took her to a clinic in the town. The doctor there tested her blood and said that she had AIDS. Mother and Father were so shocked and sad. However, they told no one in the family about the reason for the illness. They did not have money to buy medicine. Naomi never did tell them about the secret between her and Uncle. Nevertheless, Naomi knew that she caught the AIDS virus from Uncle.

As she lay dying on her bed in the little house back in the village, she looked at her thin, ugly body. She clasped her bony hands together. She saw the itchy rash, and she felt the sores in her mouth that stopped her from eating. Her cough shook her body. She heard the whispers of those who came to the house. She smelled the horrid stench of her constant diarrhoea. She felt so weak and helpless. If only she had said "no" to Uncle. Why, oh why, had she not said "no" to Uncle? [19]

Discussion Questions

1. Discuss as many things as possible that Naomi's parents could have done to prevent what happened to Naomi. What could they have taught her that might have helped her?

2. Discuss what Naomi herself could have said or done to help her stop Uncle.

---

[19] Based on facts from two verbal testimonies.

Chapter Three
How Does a Person Become Infected with HIV?

How does HIV get into someone's body? Large amounts of HIV are found in certain body fluids of infected people. The fluids that transmit the virus are blood, semen (the fluid that comes from the man's penis during sexual intercourse) and vaginal fluid (the wetness inside the vagina of a woman). Tears, saliva, urine, and other body fluids do *not* carry enough virus to cause infection, though it is present in small quantities in those fluids.

HIV spreads when an infected person's blood, semen or vaginal fluid touches a healthy person's blood or mucous membrane. Mucous membranes are the moist surfaces like those inside the mouth, in the lining of the eye sockets, inside the vagina and at the tip of the penis.

HIV spreads by sexual intercourse

The virus is passed by having *sexual intercourse* with an infected person. Even a single sex act with an HIV positive person can be enough to infect someone.

Across Africa, between *80 and 90 percent* of HIV infections occur this way. Most sexual intercourse in Africa is *heterosexual*. Heterosexual means sex between a man and a woman. *Homosexuality* is sex between two men or two women. There is relatively little homosexuality in Africa compared to Western Europe and North America, though if testimonies from boys' schools are to be believed, homosexuality may be becoming more common. In some countries in the western world, more than half of HIV infection occurs through homosexual activity. Homosexuality is forbidden by God in Scripture (Leviticus 18:22; Romans 1:21–32), just as heterosexual activity outside marriage is also forbidden.

HIV is present in the semen. Semen is the fluid that comes from  a man's penis during the act of sexual intercourse. HIV is also present in the vaginal fluids. The virus passes from the man to the woman through the thin lining (mucous membrane) of the vagina and cervix, or from the woman to the man through the mucous membrane at the tip of the man's penis.

There are many things that can make it easier or harder for the virus to pass between the sexual partners. Two things may be the most important. (1) The more virus there is in the body, the more likely it is to spread to the other person. (2) The virus can enter more easily when there are sores, wounds, or infection on the genitals. This is why treating other sexually transmitted diseases is important for preventing the spread of HIV.

HIV spreads from mother to baby

A mother can pass HIV directly to her baby. This is called "vertical transmission." It accounts for about ten percent of all HIV infections. About three out of every ten children born to infected mothers will become infected with HIV. If the mother has been newly infected, she is especially infectious to her baby. If she has not had a good diet, or if her immune system is already weak, or if she has malaria while pregnant, she is also more infectious to her baby. If she is taking antiretroviral drugs, the baby is less likely to be infected. The virus passes from mother to child in three ways.

In the womb before delivery

First, the virus can pass across the placenta into the unborn baby, but this does not happen often. It is most likely to happen when the woman becomes infected with HIV while she is pregnant. Malaria during pregnancy is dangerous to the mother and baby, and may increase the risk of passing HIV to the baby, so malaria prevention for the pregnant woman is quite important. Babies who are born too early (prematurely) are more at risk than babies who are born after their full term in the womb. Thankfully, God gave the mother and baby two separate blood systems; otherwise, *all* babies of infected mothers would become infected.

During the birth process

The second and most likely way for the baby to get the virus from the mother is during the birth process. The virus can be passed from the mother to the baby when the baby swallows fluid and the mother's blood during the delivery. Infection is more likely if the mother has an episiotomy (surgical cut) or a tear during delivery. The virus can then pass through the mucous membrane in the baby's mouth or eyes and into the baby's body. In addition, if the baby is delivered using instruments like forceps, and bruising occurs, the baby is more likely to become infected through the small cuts in the bruise. The newborn baby's skin is fragile. It is like fine tissue paper and even a small cut can be an open door for the virus from the mother's blood.

During breast-feeding

Finally, HIV can pass from the mother to her child through breast milk. The longer a baby is breast-fed, the higher the risk. When HIV-infected mothers breast-feed their babies for a year or more, about ten percent of the babies will become infected through the breast milk.[20]

Virus in the breast milk probably passes to the baby through the mucous membrane in the baby's mouth. If the mother has bleeding nipples or inflammation of the breast (mastitis), the virus is even more likely to pass from the

---

[20] Vyankandondera, J., S. Luchters, *et al.* Reducing Risk of HIV-1 Transmission from mother to infant through breast-feeding using antiretroviral prophylaxis in infants. 2nd IAS Conference on HIV and Pathogenesis, Paris, 2003, Abstract LB7.

breast milk into the baby. If the baby has breaks in the mucous membrane of its mouth, for example mouth sores or thrush, the baby is at even higher risk from the infected mother.

You cannot know if a baby has HIV until 18 months after birth.

As indicated in chapter seven, all babies of infected mothers are born with antibodies to HIV but not necessarily the virus itself. Therefore, it is impossible to know soon after birth whether a baby is going to develop AIDS. It can take up to 18 months before some of the babies lose all the antibodies they received from their mothers. Only then will their HIV test be negative. Infected babies continue to have positive HIV tests and they go on eventually to develop AIDS.[21] They may develop serious infections and even die in the first year of life.

A mother can greatly reduce the risk of passing HIV to her baby by taking antiretroviral treatment near the time of delivery.[22] When the mother and baby are treated with antiretroviral drugs, the risk of passing HIV to the baby may become lower than one in ten. That is, only one in ten babies or fewer may become infected at birth with HIV. Without such drugs the risk is closer

---

[21] Some advanced labs may be able to test for the presence of HIV virus itself, and so can make the diagnosis before six months. At present such labs are rare.

[22] In many places in Africa the drug *nevirapine* is being used, because a single tablet during labour is all that is needed. The baby is also given his own very small dose. A problem is that the HIV in the mother may then become resistant to nevirapine, making the drug less useful for her in the future when she herself needs antiretroviral therapy. As of mid 2004, we still do not know the best way to use antiretrovirals to prevent HIV from passing to the baby. Different drugs and combinations of drugs are being tested to see which are best and most practical. Your country may have a national policy on which drug(s) to use and for how long.

to one in three or four babies. However, remember that babies may also be infected later through breast-feeding.

The risk of infection is further reduced if the baby is delivered by caesarean section (surgically), and if the mother does not breast-feed the baby.

Should HIV-infected mothers breast-feed their babies?

To date there is no simple answer to this question. In some situations it will be better for the HIV-infected mother to breast-feed, while in other situations it will be better if she does not.

The United Nations Children's Fund (UNICEF)[23] says that HIV-infected mothers should avoid all breast-feeding only when replacement feeding is

- Acceptable: the mother is willing to use the alternative method of feeding; the family and others will not reject the mother because of it.
- Practical: There is enough clean water, a reliable supply of baby formula, and so on.
- Affordable: the family has enough income to buy *enough* baby formula, without taking away from the other children.
- Sustainable: the family has money, time, opportunity and energy to *continue* this feeding method.
- Safe: the mother must *understand* how to prepare the feeds (mixing correctly and using clean water and containers). She must be *able* to follow the instructions. She must be *devoted* to following the instructions properly.

---

[23] UNICEF, *HIV and Infant Feeding*, 2002.

If these standards are not *all* met, then mothers should breast-feed. It is true that there is a risk of infecting their babies with HIV. But if they do not breast-feed, there is an increased risk of the babies dying from diarrhoea and other diseases. Many mothers cannot afford tinned milk formula for their babies, nor do they have access to safe water. If the formula is mixed incorrectly or is left too long, if the water is not clean, if the cup is not washed well enough, the result may be disastrous for the baby. In truth, the above standards are rarely met in most areas of Africa, so breast-feeding will usually be the best choice. Some churches and support groups may want to consider helping the family provide artificial feeds in a way that meets the above requirements. This will help protect the baby from becoming infected with HIV.

If the HIV-infected mother becomes too weak, it is best to look for a substitute mother to breast-feed (nurse) the baby. If this is impossible, the baby must be fed artificial milk (formula), but with care to use only boiled, clean water to mix the feed. Use a cup and spoon, not a feeder or bottle. Be sure to wash the cup and spoon well after feeding the baby. You can make a nourishing pap or porridge for older babies and adults. Grind together 2 cups of groundnuts, 4 cups of guinea corn, and 2 cups of soya beans and cook them into porridge.

Decreasing the risk of breast-feeding

There are some things that make breast-feeding safer for babies of HIV-infected mothers:[24]

- Shorten the duration of breast-feeding. The mother may want to breast-feed only five or six months rather than

---

[24] UNICEF, *HIV and Infant Feeding*, 2002.

12–24 months. The baby still benefits from the early breast-feeding and the risk of HIV is much less.

- The breast-feeding mother should give the baby *only* breast milk and nothing else, especially during the first three months. She should not give her baby any water, artificial feed, pap, or other food or liquid since these may make it easier for HIV in breast milk to enter the body.

- Prevent and treat breast problems. Cracked nipples and breast infections (hot, painful breast) are more likely to pass HIV to the baby.

- Prevent HIV infection in breast-feeding mothers. A baby is in the most danger if the mother becomes infected (that is, gets HIV for the first time) during the months she is breast-feeding.

- Treat sores or thrush in the infant's mouth early. Sores in the mouth are doors for the virus to enter the body.

- Consult with a doctor or HIV treatment centre about the possibility of antiretroviral drug therapy for the breast-feeding mother, the baby, or both. As of the time this book was written, we think this might be effective and practical in some situations, but it is too early to know for sure.

HIV is passed by infected blood transfusions

HIV-infected blood transfusions cause about five to ten percent of all HIV infections in Africa. If a person receives a transfusion of HIV-infected blood, he is sure to develop the infection.

Many hospitals and clinics still do not have kits or supplies for testing blood for HIV. They may lack money to buy testing kits, or may not have a trained technician to perform the tests. Some do not understand the seriousness of the problem.

Some hospitals and clinics still give blood transfusions without testing the blood. Some governments have made the transfusing of non-tested blood an illegal act. Still, not nearly enough has been done in many rural areas to make the blood supply safe.

Please note that you are not at risk of being infected by HIV when you *give* your blood for transfusion to another person, as long as a new needle is used. You are at risk only when you receive blood from someone else.

As we saw earlier, the HIV blood test does not become positive until one to three months after infection (in some cases up to six months). During this window period, the blood will pass HIV to anyone who receives it, even though it appears safe. Therefore *there is always some danger in receiving a blood transfusion.* Blood transfusions should be avoided except when necessary. When a transfusion is truly needed, only tested blood should be used.

HIV is passed by sharing needles

Needles and syringes can pass HIV from one person to another by carrying infected blood. The risk is also great when we share needles in our clinics or pharmacies. Some well meaning people will take sick people to the back of their small shops and give them an injection of chloroquine or other medicine. When they do this with the same needle, they are sharing HIV among the people they inject. Intravenous drug abusers often share needles and syringes without sterilising them. The social problem of drug abuse is increasing among young people, especially in the big cities. Those who inject themselves using shared needles are likely to get HIV.

HIV is passed by sharing other sharp instruments

Razors and instruments used for tribal markings and circumcision can pass the virus just as needles do. They become infectious[25] when they cut the skin of an infected person and contact his blood. If the barber accidentally cuts the skin of an infected person before you, the razor could carry HIV into you if it cuts you or touches an open wound that you already have. Even so, the risk is small, and few people will get HIV even after such a prick or cut.[26] A very small percentage of HIV is transmitted this way. Infection by non-sterile blades, sharp instruments and needles accounts for only about five percent of all HIV infections.[27]

Risk to health workers

The virus can enter a health worker's body through cuts on the hands when he or she is cleaning a wound of an infected person, delivering a baby from an infected mother, doing a circumcision or taking blood from an

---

[25] That is, they can pass infection.

[26] The risk is reckoned to be as little as one infection passed for every 250 cuts or pricks. The actual risk depends on factors such as the amount of infected blood on the blade or needle and the depth of the injury.

[27] Dr Patrick Dixon, *The Truth About AIDS*, Kingsway Publications, 1994. Used with permission.

HIV carrier. Blood splashed into the eye can also infect a health worker. So can a prick with a needle with blood on it. Surgeons are most at risk. Such accidents account for only a small percentage of HIV infections. The risk of infection from a single accident is quite small, but the risk is real for a health worker who may be pricked or cut many times over the years.

How long does the HIV virus survive outside the body?

Although HIV may theoretically remain infectious for a long time outside the body, this is of little practical importance. Apart from needle sticks and cuts from sharp instruments as discussed above, extremely few, if any, infections occur from HIV outside the body. Dr Patrick Dixon writes:

It has often been said that the HIV virus is fragile and cannot survive, except at body temperature, for more than three minutes. It has also been said that it cannot withstand drying. These statements are now known to be wrong. Many people with the disease "haemophilia" (a clotting disorder) were infected by the AIDS virus, when filtered extracts of a congenitally missing protein, Factor 8, were taken from several thousand blood donors, and were freeze dried and stored, and then made up into a liquid again (with sterile water) for injection. Freezing or drying did not kill the AIDS virus. Today the Factor 8 is now heat treated for safety. An important paper in the *Journal of the American Medical Association (JAMA)* in 1986 shows that although most virus particles do become damaged after a few hours outside the body, a few may survive after 3 to 7 days in dry dust, and over two weeks in water. This study was repeated and documented in the *Journal of Medical Virology* in 1991. It was found that 1/2 of the viruses survived in water for 30 hours, and 1/4 for 60 hours. This survival rate was reduced by drying. Very large amounts of viruses in infected blood were used in these experiments. Although it is alarming to think that HIV may sometimes remain active outside the body, cases where this has resulted in infection are almost unknown and confined mainly to puncturing of the skin with blood-covered medical instruments and other accidents. *The general rule still holds true that outside of sex, and blood transfusions, the risk of HIV is very low. NO patient is known to have contracted AIDS from touching dried blood.*[28]

When we speak about AIDS, we are aware that many in the audience have ungrounded fears about AIDS. They like to think and talk about those *rare situations posing very slight risk,* rather than absorbing the truth that avoiding sex before and outside marriage and avoiding untested blood transfusions will remove almost all their risk of getting HIV infection.

Discussion Questions

1. How can you learn what your community or church wants to know or needs to know about AIDS?
2. Given that 90 percent of HIV infection is spread by sexual activity, why is it important to see what the Bible says about sexual relations?

---

[28] Dr Patrick Dixon. *The Truth about AIDS.* Kingsway Publications, 1994. Used with permission.

Ruth's blood transfusion

Joshua's wife Ruth went into labour with their third child. During the delivery, she lost a lot of blood. The doctor told Joshua that Ruth needed a blood transfusion to save her life. Joshua rushed to his brother John and asked him to give blood for Ruth. The laboratory technician tested John's blood and it was HIV negative. Therefore, his blood was given to Ruth.

After the blood transfusion, Ruth was much better and was discharged from hospital. She and her baby seemed well.

About six months later, Ruth started to lose weight, and seemed to be continuously sick. The doctor tested her blood for HIV and discovered that she was HIV positive.

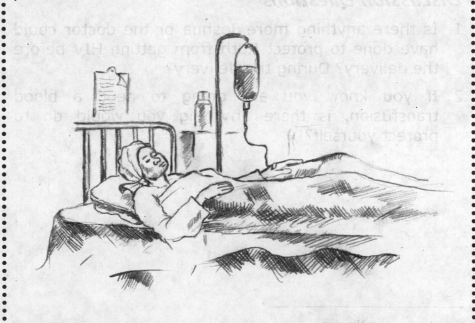

But where had Ruth got the virus? She knew that she had always been faithful to her husband. Joshua was also tested and he was found to be HIV negative. But when the doctor asked Ruth whether she had ever had a blood transfusion, she said yes. John, her husband's brother, had given her blood. John was tested and found to be HIV positive.

John had indeed given Ruth the virus. But why had his test been negative when he gave the blood? Because he had been in the window period. He had become infected only two months before giving the blood and his body was not yet producing many antibodies to HIV. His test was still negative even though his blood was full of virus. Ruth died within two years of being infected by the transfusion, leaving her husband to care for their three children.[29]

Discussion Questions

1. Is there anything more Joshua or the doctor could have done to protect Ruth from getting HIV before the delivery? During the delivery?

2. If you know you are going to need a blood transfusion, is there anything you would do to protect yourself?

---

[29] A true story from Nigeria

Chapter Four
How Can You And I Avoid Getting AIDS?

Keep sex for marriage

The best way to avoid getting AIDS is *"NO SEX BEFORE MARRIAGE, NO SEX OUTSIDE MARRIAGE."* There is no doubt that this is the most excellent way to avoid AIDS. Moreover, it is God's way.

When a man and woman marry, are both virgins, and neither has had an infected blood transfusion, they are extremely unlikely to have become infected with HIV. Therefore they cannot give HIV infection to each other. Moreover, as long as both partners in the marriage have sexual intercourse only with each other, there is no risk of acquiring HIV by sexual activity.

In Uganda, the slogans, "Love Faithfully" and "Zero Grazing" are used to describe this faithful relationship between husband and wife.

Consider Josh McDowell's words from *Why Wait?*

> Today if you have sexual intercourse with a woman, you
> are not only having sexual intercourse with her, but with
> every person that woman might have had intercourse
> with for the last ten years and all the people they had
> intercourse with![30]

*When you have sexual relations with someone, you are exposed
to all the germs that they have collected from their other sexual
partners.*

Commercial sex workers, previously called prostitutes, have a
higher risk of infection than others. Recent figures show, for
example, that in the major urban areas (cities) of South Africa
and Ghana, half the sex workers have HIV. In Nigeria and
Kenya, the figure is 30 percent.[31] In short, anyone who has sex
with a sex worker in Africa, even one who looks perfectly
healthy, is likely having sex with an HIV-infected person.

As an argument for young people having sex before marriage, I
have been asked this question several times.

"I have heard of a girl who did not have monthly periods
(menses) and she went to the doctor. The doctor's advice was
that she needed to have sex to 'open her up.' Surely you cannot
tell this girl that she should not have sex?"

In rare cases, the opening to a girl's vagina is covered by a thin
membrane called an "imperforate hymen." Having sex is *not* the
answer to this problem. A doctor can do a simple procedure for
her to let the menses out, and this will not put her at risk from

---

[30] Josh McDowell, and Dick Day, *Why Wait?* Here's Life Publishers, 1987.

[31] UNAIDS, *Report on the Global HIV/AIDS Epidemic 2002.*

HIV. Going against God's laws can never be the answer to a medical problem.

Avoiding dangerous blood transfusions

Test all blood before transfusion

The second most important way to avoid being infected by HIV is to be sure that all blood is tested before being given to a patient. It is best to avoid receiving a blood transfusion altogether unless it is truly necessary. Remember that if the donor has only lately become infected by HIV, the blood will not show HIV positive until after some weeks (see previous section on page 43 about the *window period*).

Use blood from volunteer donors

Blood given by volunteers is safer than blood that is bought. So if you or someone in your family needs a blood transfusion, it is better to ask a relative or friend whom you trust to give the needed blood, rather than allowing the hospital to go out to buy blood in the market or taxi park.

Give yourself your own blood

In some large hospitals with good power supply, patients can give blood for themselves! It is possible to give your own blood a month prior to planned surgery. The body rebuilds the blood supply during the month before surgery, and the stored blood can be used if necessary during surgery. Donating your own blood means that there is no risk of getting an infection from someone else's blood.

Prevent the need for transfusions

The need for emergency blood transfusions would be greatly reduced if every pregnant mother had a plenty of good food to eat and took iron supplements. This is something rural clinics and churches can teach pregnant women, and Bible schools can teach their students. Women may lose too much blood when giving birth. Well-trained birth attendants and midwives can do much to prevent this blood loss. Other reasons people need blood transfusions are related to poverty, poor nutrition, intestinal worms, and lack of good health care during pregnancy. All of these are causes that could be prevented.

One man, one needle; one man, one blade

It is very important that there should be *no sharing* of sharp, skin cutting or piercing instruments, in order to avoid the mixing of blood from one person to another. Thus the slogan, *one man, one needle; one man, one blade.*

Avoid injections

I knew a young woman who died from AIDS though she was a virgin and had never received a blood transfusion. She was likely infected by a shared injection needle. How tragic. *It is better to use any medicine in tablet or capsule form where at all possible, instead of taking injections.* Most modern medicines are quite effective taken by mouth. Many people mistakenly

think that an injection is better than a tablet. As long as the person is not vomiting, most medicines taken by mouth are just as effective. However, if the person must have an injection, a new syringe and needle are essential and cost little. This is a small cost to pay to protect a loved one or yourself from HIV.

Avoid drug abuse

We need to teach our young people to avoid drug abuse of any kind. Injectable drugs like cocaine and heroin are available in many of our cities, and young people are becoming addicted and killing themselves with these drugs. Shared needles often pass HIV infection from one to the other.

Use sterile instruments for cutting and injecting

Use *only* sterile instruments whenever your skin needs to be cut or pierced. Common disinfectants like Savlon and Dettol are not strong enough to kill the virus. Chemicals that do kill HIV are iodine 2%, household chlorine bleach in a 10% solution with water, rubbing alcohol 70%, surgical spirit 70%, hydrogen peroxide 6%, and Lysol 3%. Boiling instruments for 20 minutes in water also kills the virus.[32]

The best way to reduce the risk of infection from the barber's blades is to take your own new blade to the barber. That way you can be sure that there is no risk of HIV. If you absolutely cannot take a new blade, then you should insist that the barber clean his blades with a 10–20 percent bleach solution. You can make this solution using one spoonful of *fresh* bleach and five spoonfuls of water. You can even take a little bottle of this bleach solution along with you to the barber and watch him clean his blades with it before shaving you or cutting your hair. Some barbers use fire from a cigarette lighter or burner to sterilise their blades, or they use surgical spirit. These methods

---

[32] Dr Patrick Dixon, *The Truth about AIDS*, Kingsway Publications, 1994. Used with permission.

also kill any viruses that may be present. Still, the safest method is to use a new blade.

It is also important to use only a sterile blade for male circumcision. Insist that the person circumcising your baby boy use a new blade. It is best not to allow female circumcision at all. This is a cruel practice that is a health risk to women, causes them to have no pleasure in sex, and makes childbirth more dangerous for them.

"If bleach kills the virus, why do people with AIDS not drink bleach so that they kill the virus in their body?" The answer is that bleach only kills HIV by chemically damaging it, the same way it can chemically damage your body. If enough bleach reached the blood cells to kill the HIV, it would also kill the blood cells and the rest of the body's cells. Drinking bleach would be like trying to use fire to burn out the HIV from the inside of the body.

Avoiding HIV infections in the case of rape

In rape, someone forces another person to have sex against her will. Rape can spread HIV if the rapist is infected with the virus. With the increase in violent crime, including armed robbery, sadly, women and girls often have no choice but submit to rape. But at other times, there are things that they can do to protect themselves from being in a rape situation.

Women and girls need to avoid situations that leave them open to being raped. These are some examples:

- Do not be alone with strangers.
- Do not walk alone on quiet roads, especially at night.
- Avoid going to a man's room or house when no one else is there.
- Be honest from the beginning of your relationships with boys or men, by saying that you do not want to have sex.

- Pay attention to your feelings; when a situation becomes uncomfortable you should leave quickly.
- Dress modestly. Sexually suggestive dressing by women and girls never ever excuses rape. It is a fact, however, that some men think that when a girl is dressed immodestly she is really asking for sex. Some men can be sexually aroused by the sight of females in tight clothes or clothes that only cover small areas of their bodies.
- Avoid allowing men to touch you in a sexual way. Tell them immediately that you do not like it, and if possible, leave at once accompanied by a friend. Sadly, some men do not respect women or girls enough to believe that when they say "No" it means "No."

The woman being raped is especially vulnerable to infection because of bruising and damage to the mucous membrane of the vagina. This creates an open door for the virus to pass from the man's semen to the woman. The following advice, developed from experience in South Africa, may be useful to a woman in a rape situation.

- Unless you can easily attract someone's attention by making a lot of noise, or can run and escape, it may be better not to fight the rapist as this simply makes it more likely that he will hurt you more and possibly even kill you.
- If you cannot prevent the rape, spit on your hand as much as you can and put that saliva (spittle) inside your vagina before the rapist enters you. In rape situations your vagina is usually dry, which can cause tears or cuts when a man forces himself into you. The spittle will act as a lubricant and make it less likely that you will be cut and bruised.
- Report the rape to the police authorities.

- If possible, immediately get to a hospital where there are antiretroviral drugs and insist that you talk to a doctor about possible HIV-preventive treatment. The risk of getting HIV depends on factors such as who the attacker was, how the rape was carried out, and what injuries you received. If there is significant risk then you should start a course of antiretroviral drug (or drugs) immediately. This could prevent you from being infected with HIV, but only if it is used within hours of the rape.[33] You then need to continue taking antiretroviral drugs for four weeks, under the care of a doctor who knows how to use them.
- Go to a place where you can get good counselling help.[34]

Avoid drugs and alcohol

Can alcohol cause AIDS? In a way, yes! Drunkenness and alcohol abuse lead to risky sexual behaviour, bringing an increased risk of AIDS. The same is true of other substance abuse. It is obvious that people who take excess alcohol or other drugs that cloud their minds often make foolish decisions in the area of sex. One recent study in Uganda found that people who drank alcohol at all had twice the risk of getting HIV as those who never drank it.[35]

Many young people under the influence of drugs or alcohol, or both, have sexual encounters that they do not even remember. Marijuana (Indian hemp or weed) is easily available in many places in Africa. Unwanted pregnancy and sexually transmitted

---

[33] The drugs should be started as soon as possible, certainly in the first 24 hours. After 24–72 hours they are unlikely to be effective.

[34] Thomas, *Know AIDS: All the things you want to know about HIV/AIDS.* Published by Samaritan's Purse and distributed on *Prescription for Hope* CD. Appendix 4, Page 119.

[35] Mbulaiteye, S. M., A. Ruberantwari, *et al.* Alcohol and HIV: A Study among Sexually Active Adults in Rural Southwest Uganda. *Int J Epidemiol* 29(5): 911-5, 2000.

diseases can also result. It is the responsibility of parents to train their children to avoid these pitfalls. The church also has much work to do in training its young people. Too often, these issues are ignored and seen as unspiritual, while young people are facing the temptations alone, and are dying as a result.

Treat sexually transmitted diseases promptly

Sexually transmitted diseases (STDs) cause sores, irritations and discharges that are open doors for spreading HIV. If someone does become infected with an STD, it should be treated medically at once and completely. If these diseases are not treated, the sores or discharge leave the door open for other infections, especially HIV. Most people living with HIV also have other sexually transmitted diseases. Besides increasing the risk of HIV, untreated STDs can cause sterility (barrenness) and serious illness of the whole body.

Circumcision

There is evidence suggesting that male circumcision may reduce the risk of a man acquiring HIV infection. This may be because HIV can enter more easily through the inner surface of the foreskin, and because the foreskin can sometimes be mildly injured during sexual intercourse.[36, 37] This definitely does not mean that a circumcised man is then safe from HIV.

Health workers need to be careful

Health workers are at risk of getting HIV. They need to learn to always use gloves when cleaning wounds, doing circumcisions or encountering any body fluids. Midwives and surgeons are

---

[36] Anne Bayley, *One New Humanity: The Challenge of AIDS.* SPCK International Study Guide 33, 1996.
[37] Stine, G. J., *AIDS Update 2003*. New Jersey, Prentice Hall, 2003.

especially vulnerable. Some laboratory workers seem to pay little attention to their risk from HIV and do not consistently use gloves while working with blood and other body fluids. This is foolish behaviour. Gloves should always be worn by relatives or health workers when handling and dressing a dead body.

Perhaps the government trainers of health personnel need to do more work with traditional birth attendants and community health workers. Some programmes are training traditional birth attendants to test the women for HIV by using saliva test kits, and then to give the antiretroviral drug nevirapine to the infected mothers (during labour) and their newly born babies (soon after birth). In some countries up to half of the births are helped by traditional birth attendants, so it is important that they play their part in fighting AIDS.

Schools of health need to educate community health students about AIDS, how to avoid becoming infected during the course of their work, and how to care for those with AIDS. Also, schools of health need to teach students how to promote AIDS awareness in their communities. As of 2004, AIDS is *not* a major part of their syllabus in some countries, though encouragingly it is becoming more prominent. *AIDS is the number one killer in Africa.* Schools of health need to realise this, and to address HIV from all angles. The spirit of denial rules even among health workers. There is so much more that could be done at this level.

Discussion Questions

1. The message of abstinence from sex before marriage and faithfulness inside marriage is vital for HIV prevention and also for Christian living. How can the church make this message clear, attractive and effective for young people?

2. What can you do ahead of time to prevent your family being infected with HIV because of a blood transfusion?

3. What can you do ahead of time to prevent family members being infected with HIV as a result of risky behaviour after taking drugs or alcohol?

God Uses Lydia's Tragedy to Bring Her to Faith in Him

When she was 21, Lydia left her village to go to the city to find secretarial work. She stayed in the home of her uncle, who was rarely there and did not take any interest in her welfare. Lydia was a good typist and worked for a lawyer. In her work, she met many well-dressed, married men with money to spend. Lydia was quite attractive. With the money she earned, she bought herself pretty clothes, make-up and had her hair braided in attractive styles. Often the men asked her to go out for a drink with them. Frequently, it did not end there, and she gave them the sexual pleasures they asked for.

After a few years, Lydia became sick. First, she noticed that she was always getting malaria fever or typhoid fever. She was spending a lot of her money on medicine to treat herself. Then, she started to become very thin. Soon she had painful rashes down one side of her body. The doctor called it "shingles." The shingles spread over one side of her face and into her eye. One eye became blind. The doctor tested her blood and told her that HIV had infected her, and that she already had AIDS.

She did not tell anyone, but one day her cousin saw the paper with the laboratory test result, "sero-positive for HIV." Her cousin told her uncle that Lydia had AIDS and he told her to leave his house.

Lydia was no longer beautiful to look at and the men no longer wanted her. She was away from work so much that her employer asked her to leave her job. She returned to the village. Her parents learned from the uncle in the city that Lydia had AIDS. They did not want her either. They were scared of becoming infected by AIDS. So they put Lydia on a mat in a small hut on their compound, then locked the door. Every day they opened the door, placed her water and food inside, and quickly locked the door again.

A young pastor and his wife lived in the same village. The pastor had learned about AIDS and knew that having AIDS is not a sin. He knew that no one could get AIDS by caring for someone with AIDS, as long as there is no sexual activity or mixing of blood. This couple knew what Jesus would do if he was in that village. Therefore, he and his young wife took Lydia into their home. They washed her and fed her and most importantly of all, they told her about the love of the Lord Jesus Christ for sinners. Lydia knew that she was a sinner. No one knew it better than she. However, no one had told her that God loves sinners, and that Jesus Christ took her punishment for her sin when he died on the cross. A few weeks before she died, Lydia believed the good news of the gospel, and her sins were washed away. She knew that no matter what she had done, she was going to heaven to be with the Lord Jesus Christ. She knew that he was the one who loved her so much that he died for her. She died peacefully, knowing that only her faith in Christ was saving her. She did not have any good works to offer, but knew that Jesus loved her just as she was. She died in peace. [38]

Discussion Questions

1. Do you think Lydia's beauty made her more at risk than other girls? How could she have been helped to deal with the persuasions of the men who came to her?

2. Were the pastor and his wife at any risk when caring for Lydia? If so, what risks? Would you do the same as they did? If not, why not?

3. What impact do you think the actions of the pastor and his wife made to Lydia, her family, and the community?

---

[38] Based on a true story from Nigeria

Chapter Five
Ways That AIDS Is *Not* Spread

Some of my friends, both African and others, tell me that they fear going near someone with AIDS. They stay away from the homes of people living with HIV and shrink back from touching them, fearing for their own safety. One lady told me, "I just can't even make myself shake hands with my neighbour who has AIDS." This is very sad. Ignorance and fear hold back many Christian people from caring and witnessing to people living with HIV and AIDS.

You remember that earlier in this book we said HIV is spread when an infected person's blood or sexual fluid (from the vagina or penis) touches a healthy person's blood or mucous membrane. Yet because of ignorance and fear of AIDS, some people think that they will get AIDS even from working near someone with AIDS. Others have the groundless fear that they will get AIDS from eating in a hotel where the cook is HIV-infected, or from using the same toilets as people who have AIDS.

People living with HIV/AIDS are in great need of the love of Christ and of seeing the practical outworking of that love in

their lives. Do you remember how Jesus touched the "unclean" lepers, whom no one else would touch? If Jesus Christ were here in Africa today, he would surely care for the outcasts and touch them when no one else would. Read Matthew 25:31–46 again. The message is truly astounding. Jesus teaches that when we care for others who are in great need, including the sick, we care for Jesus himself!

The good news about HIV/AIDS is that it does *not* spread from one person to another by ordinary social contact. So we know with assurance that we can move together with people who are living with HIV/AIDS without any fear of infection. We can even live beside them with no fear. We can shake their hands, hug them, play sports with them, share the same bathrooms, the same cups, plates and spoons, wear the same clothes, share the same towels, bathe in the same river, use the same combs, and still not be at risk of being infected with HIV. We can travel on public transport, sit in the same classroom, even be sneezed over by a person with HIV/AIDS and not be infected by the virus. We also know that no kinds of animals or insects spread AIDS (see page 86). Let me emphasise again. If there is no sexual contact or any exposure to blood, HIV will not be transmitted in the normal, everyday activities of daily life.

Statistics confirm that AIDS is not spread by casual contact

What if HIV were spread by casual contact, like the common cold (catarrh) or meningitis? What if it were spread by unclean food and water, as diarrhoea and cholera are? If that were true, then we would see people of all ages equally becoming infected with HIV, the way they become infected with those other diseases. However, in fact, we do *not* see that pattern.

All over Africa, surveys show that almost all those living with HIV/AIDS are in the sexually active age group. Most who die are in the 20–40 age group, mainly between 20 and 29 years of age.[39] The people who die in their twenties were infected as teenagers. The few young people in the 2–14 age group who are living with HIV are the ones who were infected with the disease from blood transfusions, from their mothers during birth or shortly afterwards, from infected skin cutting or piercing instruments or, on some occasions, from sexual abuse or rape.

These statistics confirm that HIV is not spread by casual contact. If it were spread that way, people of all ages would be getting infected equally.

---

[39] United Nations (UNAIDS) Report December 2001, Geneva, Switzerland.

If someone in your family or your village is living with HIV/AIDS, you can lovingly care for them without fear as long as they live. You know now that you can be around them and touch them without fear of HIV.[40]

Do mosquitoes spread AIDS?

Many people ask whether HIV is spread by mosquitoes. In Africa and much of Asia we are used to getting malaria, which we know is transmitted by the mosquito. However, we can rest assured that the mosquito does *not* carry HIV.

Some people argue that the needle-like mouth of the mosquito could lift the virus from one person and inject it into another.

This is not possible. The mosquito does not inject blood. The mosquito sucks out blood from a person, and that blood goes into its stomach. When it bites another person, it does not inject the first person's blood into the second person, but only saliva from its salivary glands. Mosquito saliva does not contain HIV. Unlike malaria, the virus does not develop in the mosquito and is not present in its saliva. HIV only multiplies in human cells.

What about blood on the outside of the needle-like mouth (proboscis)? Scientists tell us that this needle-like mouth is so fine that it can carry extremely little blood, not enough to cause infection. Also, the mosquito rarely bites a second person immediately after biting someone. Rather, it rests and digests its meal. All these factors show why the disease is not carried by mosquitoes.[41]

---

[40] See Chapter Fifteen, Home Care for a Person with AIDS, for more on how to care and simple precautions against contact with infectious body fluids.

[41] Centers for Disease Control and Prevention (CDC). *HIV and Its Transmission*, 2003. http://www.cdc.gov/hiv/pubs/facts/transmission.htm

Statistics confirm that mosquitoes do not spread AIDS

Mosquitoes bite most people in Africa, adults and children. Everyone in Africa is bitten by mosquitoes and gets malaria— old and young alike. If mosquitoes did carry HIV, then the children and old people would also be getting HIV as well as malaria. In some parts of Africa one-quarter of young adults are HIV-infected, but even in those places children do *not* contract HIV unless they have had infected blood transfusions or unsafe injections, or received HIV from their mothers. Likewise, few elderly people are infected. If mosquitoes spread HIV as they do malaria, we would see HIV in many children and in the elderly, but we do not find this. This shows that mosquitoes cannot be spreading HIV.

Discussion Questions

1. If you had a discussion group of ten people in your church to study the effects of AIDS in your community, whom would you invite? Would you invite those living with HIV/AIDS?

2. What can you do to help others understand that AIDS is not spread by social contact?

Mary and Joel

Mary was 12 years old when Joel, who was three years older, started to talk to her on the way home from school each day. Mary liked Joel very much. When she saw him coming, her heart would beat faster, and she would feel so excited. Joel was tall and handsome and had such a nice smile. Joel was already at the secondary school on a nearby road. He always seemed to have money and would buy Mary groundnuts and other snacks to eat. She would look forward to meeting him on the road outside the school. She felt proud that Joel was her friend. Often he told her that he loved her. She felt that she loved him too, but she did feel uncomfortable about how he kept touching her when they were alone. She liked to hear him say that he loved her. He suggested that they go off to the bush together after school, but inside Mary knew that they were becoming too close and she was scared to say yes. Certainly, she knew her mother and father would not like to see them touching so much. The alarm was raised in her mind. Yet she did not want to lose Joel.

One day Joel was not there when Mary came out of school. She felt sad. Then as she walked home, she saw Joel with another girl from his own school. He had his arm around this girl. The girl's name was Rebecca. Mary was shocked and disturbed. She felt so jealous inside, because she wanted Joel to love only her. How could he put his arm around anyone else?

The following day Joel was there again waiting for her outside the school. Inside her heart, Mary was pleased, but on the outside, she was still angry with him. She put her nose in the air and walked right past Joel without speaking. However, Joel ran after her.

"Why are you angry with me, Mary?" he said.

"You say that you love me, but you have another girlfriend," she replied.

"Oh, that was just Rebecca," he said. "She's a girlfriend to every boy! Nobody takes her seriously. But she is good fun as she does what every boy wants."

"What do you mean?" said Mary.

"Well, you always say no when I tell you that if you loved me you would give me sex. Rebecca says yes to every boy. She even has boyfriends who are in senior secondary."

Mary stopped right there on the road. She looked right at Joel. She thought about how Rebecca was popular with the boys. She had often seen her with many boys around her. Mary thought for a long while. Joel was looking right into her eyes. He was so handsome. Her heart was beating fast and her hands were sweating.

"I love you, Mary," he said. "And if you loved me, you would not say no to me. Let me show you how much I love you. You really are the only girl for me."

Mary longed for Joel to truly love her. She wanted to keep him as her boyfriend, too. However, as she thought, she remembered two things. Firstly, she remembered that God wanted her to wait to enjoy sex inside marriage. Secondly, she remembered what she had heard about getting AIDS from sex. She remembered how the teacher had said that the AIDS germ could pass from the boy to the girl and the girl to the boy through sex. And there standing on the road with Joel looking right into her eyes with those big soft eyes of his, she thought of the many boyfriends that Rebecca had. Now she knew that Joel had also been with Rebecca. Mary came to a decision. No, it was not worth the risk to yield to Joel. She wanted to live long and do what was right.

"Joel," she said, "I will not give you sex. I want to live long and enjoy sex in my marriage. I know that sex is not right outside of marriage, even if it feels good. I do not want to waste my life. If you really loved me, you would not ask me for sex. I do enjoy being your friend.

Why don't we go with some of the other students and watch the football game tomorrow. But it is definitely no to sex."

It was a long speech for Mary. She was still shaking when she finished what she had to say. It was not easy.

Joel just walked away. He put his hands into his pockets and walked away never looking back. It was hard to see him go. He was so handsome and it hurt to see him walk away like that. Nevertheless, in her heart, Mary knew that she had made the right decision. Inside she felt proud of herself. She knew she had done what was right. She could respect herself. She knew that her teachers, her parents, and most importantly God, would be pleased with her decision. She had not turned her back on Joel's friendship. She showed her friendship by offering to go to the football game with him, but she had made it clear that sex was out.

Discussion Questions

1. What were the main factors that influenced Mary's right decision?

2. Discuss ways that we can all make sure our young girls have (a) an understanding of AIDS, (b) the confidence to stand up to a boy's advances, and (c) a sensitive conscience similar to the one that Mary showed.

AIDS no dey
show
for face.

Chapter Six
HIV and Other Sexually Transmitted Diseases

We entered the last century with only four known sexually transmitted diseases (STDs)[42] but now we know of many more. The most common STDs are gonorrhoea, chlamydia, syphilis, trichomonas, genital warts, herpes and hepatitis B and C infections. Some of these can be transmitted in other, non-sexual ways also.

STDs make it easier for HIV to pass from one person to another. This is partly because of the open sores (ulcers) and irritations that these infections cause in the vagina and on the penis. Just as AIDS is becoming more common, other STDs are also spreading rapidly. A person with any STD should be tested for HIV. An HIV-infected person who also has a sexually transmitted disease is more likely to pass HIV to others. Also, an HIV negative person with an STD is more likely to catch HIV from a partner. An untreated STD is likely to shorten the life of a person with HIV.

---

[42] Sometimes STDs are referred to as STIs (sexually transmitted infections) and sometimes as VD (venereal disease). An infection leads to a disease.

The following signs may *mean that a person has a sexually transmitted disease*

- Bumps, sores, blisters or warts near the genitals or mouth (often due to herpes or genital warts)
- Itching or pain near the genitals
- Swelling, ulcers or redness near the genitals (may be due to syphilis, herpes, chancroid or other infections; sometimes these are painless and ignored by the patient)
- A stinging or burning feeling when passing urine, and the need to pass urine frequently
- Fever, chills, aches, and pains, with yellowing of the skin (may be hepatitis)
- An unusual discharge or smell from the penis or vagina (may be due to trichomonas, chlamydia or yeast infection; yeast can occur for other reasons and not just as an STD. There may be an unpleasant smell.)
- Vaginal bleeding other than from a menstrual period
- Deep vaginal pain during sex
- Pain anywhere between the hips and genitals in women
- Swollen "glands" (lymph nodes)

A condom does give some protection from some STDs, but less or no protection for others like genital herpes or genital warts. The best way to prevent sexually transmitted diseases is to live according to God's guidelines for sexual purity.

Many STDs can be treated with antibiotics, and early treatment can cure them completely. Others, such as genital warts, herpes, and hepatitis B are difficult to treat, and may lead to lasting suffering or harm despite treatment.

It is important to treat STDs promptly and to complete the entire course of treatment. If a person is found to have a sexually transmitted disease, his or her sexual partners should be contacted and encouraged to get the same treatment whether or not they have symptoms. It is possible to have an STD and not have symptoms. The STD patient and all the sexual contacts should be counselled to have an HIV test.

Delayed treatment for STDs may lead to long-lasting health problems, especially damage to the reproductive organs leading to infertility (childlessness). This sometimes means that a married couple cannot conceive a baby because of damage to the wife's fallopian tubes (the tubes leading from the ovaries to the womb) or to the womb itself.

Delayed treatment (or no treatment) of STDs can also lead to *ectopic pregnancy*. In ectopic ("out of place") pregnancy, the baby begins developing

> STDs are nothing to laugh at. Some have no cure.

inside the fallopian tube leading from the ovary to the womb rather than in the womb itself. It is usually caused by fallopian tubes damaged from chlamydia or gonorrhoea. This is life threatening and needs emergency surgery to save the mother's life. Not all ectopic pregnancies are caused by STDs.

Other severe conditions can follow the initial infection if it is not treated promptly. Untreated syphilis can "disappear," only to cause problems such as heart and brain damage years later. Untreated gonorrhoea can cause eye problems and blindness in newborn babies, while chlamydia from the mother can cause pneumonia in young infants.

Some STDs have no cure and may cause severe problems. Besides causing repeated episodes of severe pain in adults, genital herpes can cause fatal infection in newborns. The virus that causes genital warts can also lead to cervical cancer in women. Hepatitis B can not only cause liver damage, liver failure, and liver cancer in adults, but is also passed on from mother to baby.

All of these facts show that STDs are not to be laughed at and that neither condoms nor drugs are a complete answer. Even if people practising casual sex avoid HIV, they can still die or become continuously ill from some other dangerous disease. They can also pass those diseases to partners and children. The only answer to all these diseases is "no sex before marriage, no sex outside marriage."

As we have repeated in this book, pastors, church youth leaders and parents have a responsibility to the youth in their care to teach them to follow God's path for their lives. It is the Christian's responsibility and privilege to promote physical as well as spiritual life to all people. Pastors must continually call people back to God's way of promoting life. Casual sex is not only leading to AIDS but to much unhappiness in marriage due to infertility problems (inability to become pregnant). Many of the problems in marriages that occur because the wife is unable to become pregnant could have been prevented. Many, though not all, of these problems could have been avoided if the young people had remained sexually pure. Childlessness today is sometimes, *but only sometimes and not always*, the direct result of yesterday's sin.

Discussion Questions

1. How common do you think sexually transmitted diseases, including HIV, are in your community?

2. Do "churchgoers" practise casual sex? If so, do the church leaders know about it? Are they doing all they can to reduce it? What more could they do?

3. Is preaching about sexual purity enough to influence behaviour? What more could be done to change the behaviour of professing Christians in this regard?

"I no go fit catch am in Jesus name."

My friend introduces me to Miriam who is a tall, slender and beautiful sex worker. My guess is that she is only 21 years of age. Her eyes are bright and shining and her skin glows in the light of the window. With only a little reservation Miriam tells me she does not like what she is doing, but earns good money from the seven to ten clients she has each day.

"I enjoy new cloth for body and chop food," she confesses.

I ask her if she knows about AIDS. Her answer shocks

me. "I no go fit catch am in Jesus name." I ask her why she is risking her life by working as a prostitute. "Na only God de keep me sa," says Miriam. "Weda you get medesin for body or not, na only God de protect man pickin."

I am shocked that this pretty, young girl, who has some knowledge of Jesus, is living in disobedience to God's law, and yet is still expecting God to care for her. Moreover, I am shocked that even though she knows about AIDS, she does not seem to think that her behaviour is putting her at extremely high risk.

"I de use condom for men we no de come always, but for my real boyfriend, I no de use am. Na only antibiotic I de use not to fall sick."

Reading the surprise and concern in my eyes, she continues more confidently again, "I only allow am with men we no de sick."

I ask Miriam to sit down with me and talk, and she agrees. I explain to her that "AIDS no dey show for body!"

"Miriam," I say, "God loves you but he is not happy that you are living this way. God made sex for our enjoyment and to create children, but only inside marriage. God wants you to be faithful to one man after you wed, and for that man to love you and care for you."

Miriam laughs nervously. "I no think say God love me O,'" she says.

"Miriam, you know in your heart that you are a sinner. You know the way you are living is not the way God wants. And Jesus died for sinners. God so loved the world that he sent Jesus Christ, his Son, into the world to save everyone who believes in him. Every person, including you, needs to come to God and talk to him. You need to ask God to forgive all the bad that you have done and ask Jesus to save you. Jesus Christ took the punishment for your sins when he died on the cross. When you trust him to save you, in the eyes of God, you become clean, just as if you have never sinned. God tells us that everyone whose sins are forgiven, and who becomes a true follower of Jesus, will live forever in heaven. When God makes you his follower, he gives you the Holy Spirit to help you not to sin. Miriam, God can give you the strength you need to leave your life of sin and follow him."

Miriam looks at me with tears in her eyes, and says in a voice that fakes a careless attitude, "I no de come to Jesus. I stay here. My friends are here. Someday, I am old, I stop?"

The tears in her eyes were mirrored in my own. In my heart, I wonder how long Miriam will live. I ask Miriam to let me pray with her and she agrees. As I hold her beautiful hands with perfect painted nails, I pray for God to open her eyes to the love of God for her. I pray that God will help her to leave her life of sin. And I pray that other Christians will also talk to her about Jesus.

In my heart, I also pray that God will cause the churches in this city to reach out to these needy young women. Someone needs to reach these precious, beautiful girls who are throwing their lives away. Jesus showed love to the woman who poured perfume on his feet and washed them with her hair, and to the Samaritan woman he met at the well. They were both involved in sexual sin. Jesus delivered them from captivity to sin, condemnation and despair. I know Jesus can do the same for Miriam.

Discussion Questions

1. Miriam's good income from being a sex worker is one of the reasons she does not want to leave her work. Is there any way your church could help someone like Miriam?

2. If you were talking to Miriam today, what would you tell her about the Christian faith and about AIDS and other sexually transmitted diseases?

Chapter Seven
Where and When Did AIDS Start?

At first, it was only a few rare patients who had the doctors puzzled about their strange illnesses. Then more and more people appeared with the illness. In the early 1980s, AIDS first appeared as a real danger to the health, development and survival of millions of individuals, families and communities throughout the world. Scientists now know that HIV, the AIDS virus, had existed for many years before 1980. Today it is continuing to cause destruction worse than all the wars we have known, all the bombs that have been dropped and all the earthquakes that we have witnessed in our world.

Other disasters look pale beside the ruin caused by AIDS. An aeroplane or bus crashes, a ferry boat sinks, and the news is reported around the world instantly! Newspapers, TV and radio all send out the sad story. Yet AIDS kills more than ten thousand people each day in Africa alone. About every ten seconds one person in the world dies from AIDS and two *more* people become infected with HIV.[43] It is clear that AIDS is still on the increase. AIDS is spreading very fast and is destroying many lives and families.

The AIDS virus kills in slow motion, claiming one life after another while spreading quietly and secretly to more and more victims. As yet, there is no end in sight. Despite the efforts of many worldwide organisations and much scientific research, no cure is in sight and no useful vaccine has been found.

AIDS in Africa is at *epidemic* proportions because of the unusual numbers of people dying from AIDS. In addition, because AIDS is occurring in many different countries in Africa and throughout the world, it is now what we call a *pandemic*, a disease breaking out everywhere.

Remember our proper focus

People often ask me, "Where did AIDS come from?" They may ask the question not only for their own information, but to blame one nation or group of people for starting the AIDS epidemic. The Beacon of Hope survey done amongst TEKAN church members in Nigeria revealed some of the beliefs about the origin of AIDS. I am sure other African countries have similar beliefs.

About half of those interviewed felt AIDS was a punishment from God, but nine percent thought it came from other various sources such as white people having sex with animals like chimpanzees, or from the United States of America. Someone thought it started in dogs.[44]

---

[43] UNAIDS/WHO, *AIDS Epidemic Update December 2002*. Geneva, 2002.

[44] Beacon of Hope Survey of TEKAN-related churches, July/August 2001, unpublished. TEKAN, Jos, Nigeria.

We need to be careful that this issue of origin does not turn us away from our proper focus. It is tempting to waste precious energy and time discussing the question of where AIDS originated, when we should be using that time and energy to *fight* AIDS.

Think of a similar example of this waste of energy. You return home and find your house on fire. What will you do first, quench the fire or stand around wasting time discussing what caused it? The important thing is for you to *quench the fire*. Our vital task now is to fight AIDS before it destroys our families and nation.

With the above warning, let me give you a brief summary of the time scale of the AIDS epidemic and some recent thinking about the origin of HIV.

Theories of the origin of HIV/AIDS

"Did God make the AIDS virus?" From the first book in the Bible, Genesis, we know that God created everything and saw that it was very good. God also created human beings in his own image, with freedom to make their own choices. But the first man, Adam, did not use that freedom in a wise way. Even though God had warned that death would follow sin, Adam sinned against God by disobeying him. For that reason he came under God's curse. In this way, Adam destroyed and spoiled some of what God had made good in all of creation.

After God's curse, sin, death and disease have been in the world and have been destroying God's creation. God allows HIV/AIDS and many other diseases to make people sick and sometimes to kill. All of creation has been injured, put in "bondage to decay."[45] The person who is suffering from a

---

[45] Romans 8:20–23

sickness is not necessarily suffering because of their own fault. God has promised that one day he will make his creation new again. He will restore it to being perfect with no more sickness, sin or suffering (Romans 8:18–23).

We do not know where HIV originated, despite much investigation and many theories. Neither do we know the origin of many other new viruses like Ebola or SARS that are appearing in our world. Most scientists, however, now believe that a chimpanzee virus called SIV "jumped species" from chimpanzees and entered humans, probably in the first half of the last century.[46, 47, 48] How this could have happened is up for debate. However, we do know that in some parts of Africa people hunt and eat chimpanzees, and so there would be opportunities for humans to become infected from the animals' blood. Evidence suggests that this actually happened more than once, leading to different types of HIV.

Some people blame the production of polio vaccines using chimpanzees for enabling this jump from one species to another.[49] Scientists have carefully researched this possibility and have recently proven it false.[50]

I have heard many other speculations during the last several years of teaching about AIDS. These include the belief that HIV was manufactured in the western world to destroy Africa and Africans. Alternatively, that God invented the virus to punish

---

[46] SIV stands for simian immunodeficiency virus. SIV is found in Central African chimpanzees.

[47] Stine, G. J., *AIDS Update 2003*. New Jersey, Prentice Hall, 2003.

[48] Kanabus, A. and S. Allen. The Origins of AIDS and HIV and the First Cases of AIDS, 2004. http://www.avert.org/origins.htm.

[49] Anne Bayley, *One New Humanity. The Challenge of AIDS*. SPCK International Study Guide 33, 1996.

[50] Worobey, M., M. L. Santiago, et al. Origin of AIDS: Contaminated Polio Vaccine Theory Refuted. *Nature* 428(6985): 820, 2004.

wickedness. Or, that scientists made a mistake and let the virus escape during laboratory work. There is no evidence for any of these ideas.

We do know that HIV has been around since at least the 1950s, as a blood sample taken in 1959 from a man in central Africa has been found to contain HIV antibodies. As early as 1978, homosexual men in the United States and Sweden, and heterosexual men in Haiti and Tanzania, began showing signs of the disease that would only later be recognised as AIDS.[51] Soon, more and more cases of immune deficiency were reported in a Congolese hospital, and by 1981, doctors in Africa were reporting something they called "slim disease," which included weight loss, oral thrush and diarrhoea.[52]

The disease AIDS became obvious to medical doctors in the Western world when it appeared in homosexual men in the United States of America in 1981. Scientists isolated the virus in laboratories in the United States and France in 1983 and in Kenya in 1984.

Whatever the origin of HIV, it is clear that the infection leads to AIDS and early, often painful, death. There is still no cure for AIDS, which is now the leading cause of death in Africa. A recent US intelligence report states that because of the predicted global impact during the next decade, HIV/AIDS is a major threat to the national security and economic development of sub-Saharan African countries, as well as to some other countries.[53]

---

[51] So Little Time ... An AIDS History. AEGIS, 2001. http://www.aegis.com/topics/timeline/

[52] Anne Bayley, *One New Humanity. The Challenge of AIDS.* SPCK International Study Guide 33, 1996.

[53] *HIV/AIDS as a Security Issue.* International Crisis Group, Washington/Brussels, 2001, and *The Global Infectious Disease Threat and Its Implications for the United States,* US National Intelligence Council, 2001.

Discussion Questions

1. Discuss whether it is important to know how and where AIDS started. Why or why not?

2. What can we do to help people to move beyond fruitless speculation and keep our focus on how to fight the AIDS epidemic?

Psalm 60, the AIDS Psalm

(an African Paraphrase)

Psalm 60, the AIDS Psalm
(an African Paraphrase)

You have rejected us, O God, and broken our bodies.

    You have been angry with us; now restore us to your favour.

You have shaken Africa and split it open.

    Seal the cracks before it completely collapses.

You have been very hard on us,

    making us drink wine that sent us reeling.

But you have raised a banner for those who honour you—

    a rallying point in the face of attack.

Use your strong right arm to save us,

    and rescue your beloved African people.

God has promised this by his holiness:

    "I will divide up Africa with joy.

    I will measure out the Rift Valley.

Mozambique is mine,

and Burkina Faso belongs to me.

South Africa will produce my missionaries,

And Nigeria will produce my bishops.

Your bodies will continue to be my servants,

. and your immune systems will once again be my slaves.

I will shout in triumph over the cemetery."

But who will deliver us from HIV?

Who will give us victory over AIDS?

Have you rejected us, O God?

Will you no longer walk with our people?

Oh, please help us against this great enemy,

for all human help is useless.

With God's help we will do mighty things,

for he will trample down this mighty foe.

By Danny McCain,[54] based on the *New Living Translation*

---

[54] Dr Danny McCain, Associate Professor, Religious Studies Dept, University of Jos.

Chapter Eight
HIV: How Big Is the Problem Already?

When we discuss statistics about how many people have HIV/AIDS, it is easy to forget that behind each of these figures there is a person and family who are experiencing great suffering. Let us remember this. As I heard one man say recently, "A statistic means nothing. However, when my son died from AIDS, it was a nightmare and a tragedy. It has given me a whole new outlook on the suffering that AIDS brings into a family." I often say statistics about AIDS are "numbers with the tears washed off."

United Nations Secretary General Mr Kofi Annan, who is from Ghana, says, "We must make people everywhere understand that the AIDS crisis is not over; that this is not about a few foreign countries far away. This is a threat to an entire generation; this is a threat to an entire civilization."[55]

---

[55] CAFOD: *AIDS Information Exchange Newsletter*, April 2001.

As we write in the year 2004, it is 23 years since the AIDS epidemic was recognised as a threat to the survival of millions. In those 23 years, 65–70 million people have been infected and 25 million have already died.[56] In comparison, all the wars in the 20th century killed perhaps 33 million soldiers.[57]

Shocking facts about the extent of AIDS in Africa

- Forty-two million people are living with HIV/AIDS worldwide and 29.4 million of them are in sub-Saharan Africa.
- There are now 16 countries in Africa in which more than one in ten adults (aged 15–49) is infected with HIV. In seven countries, all in the south, at least one adult in five is living with HIV.
- Worldwide, thirteen million children are living as orphans because of AIDS. Eleven million of them are in sub-Saharan Africa.
- By 2010, twenty million children in sub-Saharan Africa will have lost one or both parents to AIDS. By then *15–25 percent* of all the children in a dozen of these countries will be orphans, mostly due to AIDS.
- Two-thirds of all people living with HIV/AIDS are in sub-Saharan Africa, though only ten percent of the world's population live there.
- Ninety percent of those living with HIV/AIDS are not aware that they have contracted the illness.

---

[56] Idemyor, V. 20 Years since Human Immunodeficiency Virus Discovery: Considerations for the Next Decade. *Pharmacotherapy* 23(3): 384-7, 2003.

[57] Unpublished remarks by Dr Helen Gayle, HIV/AIDS senior advisor to Bill and Melinda Gates Foundation, at Prescription for Hope Conference, Washington, DC, February 2002.

- Many, if not most, African women living with HIV/AIDS were infected by their husbands.
- Infection rates in young African women are far higher than in young men. In some African countries, the rate of infection in teenage girls is four times that of boys.
- 800,000 African children were newly infected with HIV in the year 2001.
- 3.5 million Africans were newly infected in 2002.
- If things continue as they are now, about *half* of the adolescent boys now living in South Africa or Zimbabwe will die from AIDS. In Botswana, where nearly forty percent of adults are infected, *two-thirds* of the adolescent boys will die of AIDS unless something major changes.
- In Eastern and Central Europe, one million are infected.
- In Western Europe, half a million are infected.
- Ninety-five percent of new infections are in developing countries.
- Of the 14,000 new infections daily, there are 2,000 new infections in children under 15 years old, and 12,000 in the 15–49 age group.
- In the last twenty years, AIDS has killed ten times more people than all of the wars in Africa in the last one hundred years.
- In six countries of southern Africa, AIDS is expected to claim the lives of eight to twenty-five percent of today's practising doctors within a few years.[58]

---

[58] UNAIDS Reports from June 2000, 2001; *UNAIDS AIDS Epidemic Update*, December 2002 and December 2003; *Report on the Global HIV/AIDS Epidemic* (UNAIDS/02.26E) UNAIDS, 2002; *USAID Report* 2001, UNAIDS Facts Sheets "AIDS and Population" and "HIV/AIDS in Africa," *Africa's Orphaned Generations* (UNICEF 2003), and World Bank Report 2000.

> AIDS is wiping away the last century's advances in many areas of life.

Life expectancy is the average length of life in a country. The life expectancy in many African countries is decreasing because of the AIDS epidemic. In the four worst-affected countries in southern Africa (Botswana, Malawi, Mozambique and Swaziland), the average life expectancy has dropped to 40 years. In all of sub-Saharan Africa, average life expectancy has dropped from 62 years (where it should have been by now) to 47 years. In other words, the average person is expected to live only 47 years, because of the impact of HIV.[59]

AIDS is wiping away the last century's advances in many areas of life. All over sub-Saharan Africa, teachers and students are dying or leaving school, reducing the quality of education. In 1999 alone, an estimated 860,000 children in sub-Saharan Africa lost their teachers to AIDS.[60] In the Central African Republic, AIDS was the cause of 85 percent of the teacher deaths that occurred in 2000.[61]

Also in Zambia, teacher deaths from AIDS are equal to about half the total number of new teachers the country manages to train annually.[62]

In several southern African countries the government has banned burials every day of the week apart from Saturday. This is to avoid the disturbance of life by the daily burials.

---

[59] *HIV/AIDS, Human Resources and Sustainable Development* (UNAIDS/02.48E). UNAIDS, 2002.

[60] UNICEF press release, 28 November 2000.

[61] *HIV/AIDS Leading Cause of Death for Teachers*. UN Integrated Regional Information Network, 2001. http://www.aegis.com/news/irin/2001/IR010901.html

[62] UNAIDS Report December 2001, Geneva, Switzerland.

As reported above, there now 16 countries in Africa where more than one-tenth of the adults are infected with HIV, and seven countries where at least one adult in five is living with the virus. In Botswana 39% of adults are infected, in Lesotho 31%, in Swaziland 33.7%, in South Africa more than 20%, and in Zimbabwe 34% of adults are infected.[63]

In West Africa, Cameroon has an adult infection rate of 12%, Ivory Coast 10%, Nigeria 6%, Ghana 3%, and Benin 4%. Some East African examples include Kenya (15%), Ethiopia (6%), and Tanzania (8%).[64]

On a brighter note, Uganda is the first African country to begin subduing a major HIV/AIDS epidemic.[65]

Although young girls are especially vulnerable to the epidemic, millions of them are dangerously ignorant about HIV/AIDS. According to UNICEF, more than 70 percent of adolescent girls in two West African countries have never heard of AIDS.[66]

---

[63] UNAIDS Report December 2002, Geneva, Switzerland.

[64] *Report on the Global HIV/AIDS Epidemic* (UNAIDS/02.26E). UNAIDS, 2002.

[65] "HIV prevalence in pregnant women in urban areas has fallen for 8 years in a row, from a high 29.5% in 1992 to 11.25% in 2000. Focusing heavily on information, education, and communication, and decentralized programmes that reach down to the village level, Uganda's efforts have also boosted condom use across the country. Uganda's experience underlines the fact that even a rampant HIV/AIDS epidemic can be brought under control. The axis of any effective response is a prevention strategy that draws on the explicit and strong commitment of leaders at all levels, that is built on community mobilization, and extends into every area of the country." UNAIDS Report December 2001, Geneva, Switzerland.

[66] Ibid.

East, Central and Southern Africa

An example of the social and financial ruin brought by AIDS

AIDS is steadily breaking down the health, economic and social structures of countries throughout sub-Saharan Africa. The health costs are already great and are constantly rising. In large hospitals in East, Central and Southern Africa up to *half of all patients in hospital suffer from AIDS-related illnesses.* AIDS is creating grief beyond measure.

A study in Rwanda showed that families with HIV-infected members spent on average $63 for health care, compared to only $3 per household without HIV.[67]

Often, the illness or death of a family member leads to a large reduction in family income. This affects many people. There is less money to buy food, less money for fertiliser for the farm so a smaller harvest, and less money for school fees. So, there is a fall in the nutrition of families. In this way, HIV is causing lasting damage even to children who are not infected.[68] The children become malnourished and more open to sicknesses, including HIV infection.

Many children do not attend school because of the sickness or death of wage earners in the family. They often have to work at home, farming and caring for their siblings. One study in Central African Republic shows that only 39 percent of orphan children attend school, compared with 60 percent of other children.[69] The education sector is also affected by the loss of

---

[67] Scheider *et al.*, 2000. Paper presented at IAEN symposium, 2000.

[68] Leonie McSweeney, *A Challenge to Love...Changing Behaviour.* Ibadan. Ambassador Productions.

[69] UNICEF Report 1999.

teachers who have AIDS. In Botswana, four percent of all children have lost a teacher to AIDS.[70] Estimates in 2000 were that 12 percent of all educators in South Africa were infected with HIV.[71] Girls are suffering most, because if there is money to send children to school, the boys in the family are usually the ones who are privileged to attend.

AIDS is making poverty wider and deeper and inequality much worse. The store of knowledge that societies have collected is also being lost as many well-educated leaders, thinkers, writers, and experienced, wise people are also dying. Governments, civil service, the courts, and the armed forces are all feeling the effects of leaders dying from AIDS.

HIV also decreases productivity in industry. Many workers are sick. Companies are being crippled by high absenteeism, having to train new workers, paying pensions and sickness allowances, and helping with the cost of burials. Some employers are paying for antiretroviral drugs for their HIV positive workers, believing that it is economically better for them to keep their existing workers alive and healthy than to have to train new skilled workers.

Dr L. McSweeney is a medical doctor who has worked both in East Africa and in Nigeria. She writes,

> I believe that we have much to learn from East African countries and indeed the world owes a debt of gratitude to their leaders. They have opened up the tragic experience of their people so that those in other parts of the world might learn from their suffering. While visiting India one government minister from East Africa gave the following advice at a public address: "Take heed of our

---

[70] UNICEF/UNAIDS Report 2000.
[71] Coombe. C., quoted in UNAIDS Report 2000.

experience. When AIDS hit us we did not have the advance warning and knowledge that you have."[72]

Society's young adults, who are the most productive in supporting the family and the economy, are being destroyed. AIDS is steadily weakening the extended family system, which for generations has been an effective means of coping in times of crisis. In East, Central and Southern Africa, you may go to villages where only the old people and young children remain. Almost all the young adults are gone, and elderly grandparents are struggling to care for their orphaned and often sick grandchildren.

Dr L. McSweeney writes about orphans:

> I met one grandmother who looks after 35 grandchildren. She had lost 23 of her children, including their spouses. Later I saw another grandmother who showed me 13 graves of her children who had died from AIDS. In a nearby area, 75% of children had lost either one or both parents.[73]

Beyond Africa

HIV/AIDS is not a problem in Africa alone. Although the focus of this book is largely on Africa, HIV is also spreading rapidly through other areas, especially in Asia and the former Soviet Union countries. Now is a critical time for people in those areas to act to *prevent* disaster. Here are a few examples of the grim facts:

- About 7.5 million people in Asia and the Pacific are living with HIV.

---

[72] Ibid.
[73] Ibid.

- China's Guangxi province had little HIV until 1997, but within three years, over ten percent of the commercial sex workers were infected.
- In India, around 4–5 million people are infected already. By 2010 there will probably be around twenty million infected. A recent report even says that in a few years India may have the largest number of HIV infections of any country.
- In some cities of India, more than half the commercial sex workers are infected with HIV.
- Eleven to twenty-four percent of commercial sex workers in two cities in Vietnam are infected.[74]

Discussion Questions

1. Do you think that knowing the huge numbers of deaths from AIDS recorded in these statistics is enough to change people's behaviour? Why or why not?

2. What more is needed to convince people first of all that AIDS is real and secondly that they should change their behaviour?

3. How can all of Africa and Asia learn from the course of the HIV/AIDS epidemic in Africa over the last 20 years?

[74] Sources for these statistics include: *UNAIDS AIDS Epidemic Update,* December 2003; Schaffer, T. C. and P. Mitra. *India at the Crossroads: Confronting the HIV/AIDS Challenge.* Center for Strategic and International Studies, 2004.

Salome's One Big Mistake

Salome was in senior secondary school and thinking about going to university. She was a beautiful girl and smart, too. She worked hard at school and everyone respected her. All through her school she wanted to be a doctor. She studied hard and every teacher knew that she would make it. Salome was a virgin. She had never had sex with anyone. All the boys knew that Salome was a virgin and they respected her for that. She always said no to the boys who asked her to go with them.

There was a boy in Salome's class. His name was Noah. He was very attractive. Everyone knew that Noah had many girlfriends. Just before the party at the end of the last year of school, Noah asked Salome to go with him to the party. She had always liked Noah, and as it was her last week in secondary school, Salome said yes.

On the night of the party, there was loud music and lots of close dancing, and the lights were dim. The evening was full of emotion and romance. Salome and Noah danced together all night. It was exciting. After the last dance, Noah started to walk home with Salome. Both of them felt the way they liked each other. They lusted after each other. In a dark place on the road home, they started to kiss, then to touch and caress each other all over. Without meaning to, Salome let Noah have sex with her.

Salome got the top marks in her school. She was accepted to go to study medicine at university. Her dream was coming true.

Salome studied hard in medical school. After some years, she became a doctor. In fact, she became a specialist in delivering babies and looking after pregnant mothers. She loved her job.

It was a wonderful day when she married another doctor called Adam. Salome was Adam's first girlfriend. Soon, they had a beautiful baby boy, called Jacob, and the parents and grand parents were pleased. There was a big party to celebrate the arrival of Jacob. They had a large house and were happy together. They loved each other dearly.

When Jacob was six months old, he became sick. He would not eat and started to lose weight. Salome took him to see a friend of hers who was a doctor who took care of babies. This doctor took some blood from Jacob, and when he tested it, he found that Jacob had HIV antibodies in his blood. When he told Salome she was so shocked. She wept. She must have given Jacob the HIV antibodies, which meant she must have HIV herself. Indeed, her own blood test showed she was infected. Adam's test showed that he also had HIV.

Salome's parents and grandparents and Adam's parents and grandparents could not believe this was happening in their family. Of all the people who felt the sadness, Salome was most sad. After several years, Salome, Adam and Jacob all died from AIDS.

Salome did not say *no*. She lived to regret her decision as she saw her husband and new baby suffer and die because of her few minutes of foolish pleasure.

Discussion Questions

1. Discuss how Salome and Adam's extended family must have felt when they found out that their highly successful children were infected with HIV.

2. Who do you think the family would blame? Salome? Adam? Society? Satan? God?

3. How could you as a Christian help Salome and Adam's family in their suffering?

Chapter Nine
Social Reasons for the Fast Spread of AIDS

A simple answer that is not enough

Often, as we speak to people about AIDS, they tell us that people with AIDS are paying for their sinful actions. They say AIDS is a sin. Other times, our audiences do not openly say that people with AIDS are to blame for their own suffering. Yet, by their unwillingness to be involved in fighting AIDS or caring for people living with HIV/AIDS, they are saying almost the same thing. Many people suffering with AIDS, however, did not get it through their sinful behaviour.

There is no simple answer to why AIDS is becoming such a big problem. HIV infection most often happens through sexual intercourse with an infected person. However, the process does not begin with that act of intercourse. It occurs against a background of complex social, religious, and economic factors. These conditions and circumstances, as we will see, prepare the ground for the infection.

It is true that men and women need Jesus Christ as their Saviour. It is true that if they let him be the Lord of their lives, then this lordship of Christ will go a long way along the road to solving the AIDS problem.

Yes, one of the basic reasons for the epidemic is that men and women are far from God, and are often not acting according to his plan. It is true that unless men and women know God and his saving power in their lives, they are bound by sin and will tend to continue to practise sin. But, we must understand that simply stating and believing those facts is not enough. To leave the issue there is to oversimplify the problem. Much more needs to be said.

> Nine out of ten HIV infections in Africa are caused by sexual activity.

The problems we mention here are based on our own observations of our combined 27 years in Nigeria. We are sure that you our readers can add to and correct our observations. As non-Africans, we welcome these additions, corrections and modifications. We ask you to please be patient with our interpretations of what we see around us. We are writing from a desire to see change that will save many from destruction and certainly not to criticise the people whom we love and work with.

Nine out of ten HIV infections in Africa are caused by sexual activity. Therefore, most of the factors we will discuss here are related to the sexual promiscuity that exists in our societies. Promiscuity is *not* limited to those outside the church. AIDS counselling centres often counsel church members. *"AIDS is Real and It's in Our Church,"* as well as in society in general.

Root problems

Ignorance

The proverb says, "A little knowledge is a dangerous thing." This is certainly true when dealing with HIV/AIDS. In many places, ignorance about AIDS is profound. Ignorance is one of the main reasons the epidemic is still prevailing. Early on, before AIDS has fully taken hold in an area, people tend to close their eyes and pretend it does not exist. As it becomes common, people are forced to recognise it. Because of the increasing number of burials of young adults, they begin to see that something sinister is happening. Too many people are attending burials every week not to take some notice of how many young men and women are dying. Of course, it would be far better if people recognised the truth about HIV much earlier rather than waiting for the sad evidence to be obvious.

Most HIV-infected people do not know they have the virus. Some people do know they have the virus but do not know how they got it. Many do not know how the virus is spread, and so do not know how to prevent passing it on.

The Beacon of Hope survey, carried out amongst a group of churches in Nigeria, showed that few of those surveyed had heard the truth about HIV/AIDS or attended a workshop on HIV/AIDS. Very few had had the chance to read pamphlets or books about AIDS, and not many had been informed at school. Only one in twelve people had discussed AIDS with their pastor. *No one* listed the church or the pastor as a source of information about AIDS.[75]

---

[75] Beacon of Hope Survey of TEKAN-related churches, July/August 2001, unpublished. TEKAN, Jos, Nigeria.

Certainly, more work needs to be done to inform our people about AIDS. Television, radio, car stickers and posters are making people more and more aware that AIDS is real, that it is sexually transmitted, and that it is incurable. Even so, many people do not think the risk applies to them personally. Besides, many times the little knowledge they *do* have about AIDS does not cause them to change their sexual behaviour. Many young people have the careless, reckless attitude, *"We all have to die anyway. It could be on the roads, or some other way."*

Many people feel death is unavoidable, destined, and always close, especially with sickness and road accidents taking their toll. So, they do not see the delayed risk of AIDS as any real threat to them personally. Their sexual promiscuity today does not lead to AIDS for many years to come. The behaviour and the end result seem unconnected. One young man said to me:

> "I could be dead in ten years anyway because of an accident or anything at all, so why should I worry about AIDS. I may as well have as much fun as I can before I die."

If someone who had sex with a co-worker today died from AIDS next week, the connection between the immoral behaviour and its result would be clear. The coffins would more obviously be our campaign tool. However, HIV is a slow killer. The years pass, and the results of promiscuity do not seem to be serious. It is difficult for people to understand that something that happened three, six or ten years ago could be causing death now.

False information

Those who think they do know about AIDS often have mistaken information. Sometimes they hear a myth and believe it. For example, they may believe the recent false rumour, publicised in some Nigerian papers, that a reputable multinational company has spread the AIDS virus into sanitary napkins/towels in an effort to destroy Africans. Or, they may believe the similar lie that the western nations have placed HIV inside meningitis or polio vaccinations, also trying to destroy Africans.[76]

On the other hand, some people simply believe the lie that AIDS is spread by casual social contact or mosquitoes, so that there is nothing anyone can do to stop it. Some are fatalistic in their views, saying that if it is the will of God or the will of Allah, they will die from AIDS. Because of this fatalism, they do not change their behaviour.

Some people believe that if they have sex only with healthy-looking people, they will not become infected with HIV. Many well-nourished, well-dressed, wealthy men and women are carrying HIV. A single sex act with one of them can infect you and lead to AIDS and early death.

One man mistakenly said to me, "If you have a wife, you cannot get this disease."

Many young people believe that their parents are using the fear of AIDS to stop them from having fun. They also say the acronym AIDS stands for the "American Invention to Discourage Sex." Some say the AIDS virus was introduced into Africa by the developed, western countries, either as a method of reducing the African population, or as a threat to stop people producing children. We have heard this quoted many times in the last few years.

Some also mistakenly believe that if young people use the contraceptive pill, they will not become infected with HIV. The

---

[76] BBC World Service, March 2000 and January 2004.

truth is, the contraceptive pill may prevent pregnancy, but it does not protect against HIV infection.

Due to wide advertising of condoms, many people falsely believe condoms will always prevent AIDS. In fact, the active promotion of condoms for our young people could contribute to the spread of AIDS by giving them a false sense of security and encouraging them to be sexually active. The issue of condoms is discussed later in this book.

Many still wrongly believe that AIDS is caused by a curse or witchcraft rather than believing the evidence that AIDS is caused by a virus, just as many other sicknesses are also caused by viruses.

Parents' silence

The father of lies hates the truth. One of his strongest weapons for spreading AIDS is to prevent parents talking to their children about sex. He makes them afraid or uncomfortable about talking with them. He tells them the lie that their children do not need to know, or will learn on their own.

So often we meet young people and discover that no one has ever explained to them anything about how babies are conceived, or about any of the sexually transmitted diseases, including AIDS. Many of these young people are sent off to boarding schools far from their parents.

It seems parents rarely have given their young daughters guidelines on how to handle the persuasive words of the boys and men they will meet. Likewise, most fathers have not taught their young sons how to resist the temptation to go into sexual activity, even when the girls flirt with them, or when other young men are being promiscuous.

We are leaving our young people to negotiate their relationships without guidance from the people who should be most interested in their welfare. Young people today are facing great pressures towards sexual activity. Few of their parents had to face such pressures. We simply are not helping these dear young people enough to deal with the pressures.

> We must be willing to talk about these issues if we are to save the next generation.

We have met educated parents who tell us they do not know how to talk to their children about sex and AIDS. One of these said that the nearest she came to talking to her teenagers about sex was to leave a little booklet in an obvious place, hoping her teenagers would ask her questions. The book was about a cat having kittens! The teenagers ignored the book and their unvoiced questions were never answered.

Most parents in any country, including our own, find it hard to talk about sex with their children, and so they find it almost impossible to talk about AIDS. There are no words to talk clearly about sex in a non-embarrassing way, so ignorance triumphs, and our young people keep dying. We are leaving them in darkness rather than leading them into the light.

We must be willing to talk about these issues if we are to save the next generation. In the light of AIDS, we must throw aside any hesitation or discomfort and talk directly about sex. The crisis forces us to change our ideas about what is proper to discuss with our young people. The Bible says parents need to *train* their young people in the way they should go, and that when they are old, they will not leave that way (Proverbs 22:6). Such training requires from us more than a book about cats and kittens.

Joshua was a young man dying of AIDS. I heard him describe how, when he was a teenager, his mother once beat him when some girls came to visit him in their home after a church service. He said that all he and the girls were doing was talking in the parlour. He related that he understands now, looking back, that his mother was trying to give him sex education! At the time he did not understand. Joshua went on to say that his mother did not know how to tell him the dangers of sex before marriage, and that if only she had known a better way than beating him, he might not now be dying from AIDS. How tragic.

Parents, we owe it to our children to save them from AIDS by talking with them about these things. God wants us to train our children during the years that he has given them to us. He wants us to prepare them to face the temptations outside the home.

One of the authors has written a little booklet, *Ten Great Reasons why you should say NO to sex before marriage.* This booklet may be helpful for parents or teachers to give to children and young people to educate them about the risks they face. It is available from Africa Christian Textbooks, Theological College of Northern Nigeria, Bukuru, Nigeria. It has also been translated into Hausa and French.

Cultural issues of power and gender

African culture often creates a feeling of inferiority in girls. It is not easy for them to reject a man's advances. Knowing how vulnerable young girls are, it is cruel for us to leave them without the training, knowledge and determination needed to live in a way that avoids AIDS. A young girl needs her parents, the church and the community to protect her.

The flatteries that will lead girls into trouble will sometimes come even from their teachers. They may also come from older men with cars, men who offer many delights in exchange for sexual favours. When far from home, these girls are tempted to say "yes," in exchange for food and pretty cloth.

Men who in days gone by were visiting commercial sex workers[77] now look for young girls in school, believing that they are AIDS-free. In some areas, there is a false belief that if an infected person has sex with a virgin, then the HIV will disappear.

Younger girls are particularly at risk, and sadly it is often the "good," obedient young girls who become infected with HIV. Being "good" and obedient, they do what their elders say, especially if the person giving the orders is a man. The assertive and aggressive girls are safer. They are more able to say "no."

---

[77] Previously called prostitutes, now termed commercial sex workers

If a girl "gets into trouble" with an unplanned pregnancy or a sexually transmitted disease, it is often because those who should be caring for her have left her powerless and defenceless. Yet she often carries the blame single-handedly. Christian parents and the Christian church are in the strongest position to help her avoid this tragedy, and they have the greatest responsibility to demonstrate what can be done. God's servants and Christian parents, using God's word, *must* teach their children about sex. In today's moral climate, what we teach them may well save their lives.

We need to make clear to our young people that God has created them for a high purpose and a meaningful life. There is no doubt that the most effective resistance strategies for the AIDS epidemic involve *truth* to combat the behaviour and moral ignorance that lead to death.

Shame, stigma, fear and denial

The father of lies is also the father of shame and fear. While God loves to pour out his grace and love on us, the enemy wants to cover us all with shame, telling us the lie that we are bad, useless people. He loves to create fear in us by telling us the lie that only suffering and punishment await us, and by making us doubt the love and power of God.

When people learn they are infected with HIV, they are often ashamed and frightened. They may deny their illness even to themselves and try to hide it from others. They do not want to admit their status because they could become outcasts from their families, lose their jobs, be rejected by neighbours, or even worse, be stoned and killed, as has happened in some places.

Many people view those with AIDS as disgraced, shameful, punished by God and cursed by someone. Others see infected people as tainted, soiled and without dignity or rights. Some people even suggest that the government should isolate those with HIV, perhaps in hospital. Some go so far as suggesting that infected men should be made impotent.

When asked why people do not talk freely about AIDS, respondents say things like, "It is a disease of disgrace, and the sickness will catch them if they talk about it."[78] One lady said, "My friends pretend to be sorry, and then they run away from me." In a survey of attitudes related to HIV in Ethiopia, more than 60 percent of respondents said they would never buy from a vendor with HIV.[79]

We must ask ourselves whether our attitudes and actions reflect God's grace, forgiveness and love, or something else. Consider how Jesus responded to the sick, the lepers and the sinners. By God's grace, we need to renew our minds and change our attitudes, so that those who are suffering need not feel shame and hide their sickness. If not, we are like the Pharisees who condemned "sinners" and as a result, never knew God's forgiveness.

Over recent years, we continue to hear stories of harsh mistreatment of people with HIV.

- Property owners have thrown families out of their homes because someone in the family has AIDS.
- Schools have sent children home from school because of their mother's infection.
- Employers have dismissed employees because they had HIV or AIDS.

---

[78] Beacon of Hope Survey of TEKAN-related churches, July/August 2001, unpublished. TEKAN, Jos, Nigeria.

[79] International Centre for Research on Women, "Unraveling the Complexities of HIV Related Stigma and Discrimination in Sub-Saharan Africa," November 2002.

- A high court judge reportedly stopped courtroom proceedings to determine whether it was safe to allow an HIV-infected plaintiff to enter the room.[80]

As the last example shows, even some educated people are ignorant about AIDS and how it is spread. Thus, they have added to the fears many less educated people have.

One woman told me, "Whenever I take my plate of food and go sit next to my friends, they move from the bench and I am left sitting by myself. They are all running away from me."

Another young woman said, "My mother does not bring me good food and medicines any longer now that she knows I have HIV. I can even ask for money for Panadol [paracetamol] and she will say she has none."

Many of our churches require HIV testing and pregnancy testing before marriage. Because young people want to be married in church but fear the stigma of HIV and pregnancy before marriage, some bribe laboratory staff to give false HIV and pregnancy test results. Tragically for mother and baby, some even have an abortion in order to have the negative pregnancy test needed to stand in church on their wedding day.[81]

Many of the abortions are done illegally, often with unsterile instruments which can themselves introduce HIV and other infections. The infections and the rough method used to do the abortion can lead to barrenness. How sad to take the life of your unborn child just so you could be married in church. And how

---

[80] Chinua Akukwe, "AIDS in Nigeria: The Clicking Time Bomb," 2001. http://www.afbis.com/analysis/aids_nigeria.htm. Dr Akukwe is former Vice-Chairman of the National Council of International Health based in Washington DC.

[81] Sometimes the abortion is discovered weeks later when the woman goes for the required pregnancy test and it is positive. This is because the hormones that make the test positive have still not disappeared from her body.

sad if the child you killed was the only baby you were ever able to conceive. Having a white church wedding is not worth the price.

Our church leaders need to work out policies that allow couples who have sinned sexually to come in true repentance and be accepted back into the body of Christ. Often a woman is not allowed to be part of the women's fellowship if she has not been married in church. That is a huge punishment for her. Does she have to abort her child or bribe a laboratory technician in order to be allowed back into the church fellowship where she will have the spiritual nurture that she needs? Surely there must be a better way.

Some churches have dismissed employees because of HIV infection. The church is the very place where our actions should be the opposite from what happens in the world. Having AIDS is not a sin. Many contracted it through no fault of their own, and many do not know how they were infected, but even that is not the issue. *All of us are sinners, and all have broken God's law.* None of us deserves God's love and mercy. So, why point the finger at others?

If you know you are HIV negative today, thank God for his mercy, but do not think you are more righteous than your infected brother or sister. Perhaps you, too, were involved in sexual sin in the past, maybe before giving your life to Christ. Remember, also, Jesus taught that the person who lusts commits adultery in his heart. If HIV had existed twenty or thirty years ago, or was carried by "adultery in the heart," would not many of us be infected?

Jesus and Sinners

Many of the people Jesus ate with and cared for would have been HIV-infected or at high risk if the virus had existed then.

Jesus did not shrink from them. People scornfully called him a friend of sinners (Luke 7:34). If Jesus were here, he would be caring for those with AIDS.

> Are we disciplining people for something that happened years ago?

Even if someone *did* contract HIV through a sinful act, that is no reason for stigma because Jesus loves sinners and died for them—for us![82] Forgiveness, grace and redemption are the wonderful truths of the gospel we preach. Certainly, if someone continues living in sin, he or she needs to be disciplined with the hope of restoration. But often, when the illness is discovered, the sinful life is long past and the person is married and living a life of faith in Christ. Are we disciplining people for something that happened years ago?

Is it any wonder that people who are HIV positive are afraid to tell anyone? They do not want the disgrace and exclusion attached to AIDS, and so they tell no one. Some continue as before, infecting others by their lifestyles.

Because of the shame attached to AIDS, rarely does any family admit that AIDS was the cause of a loved one's death. If you ask the family why someone died, they say it was from pneumonia, TB, or malaria. Then again, they may say, "It is an attack. Someone put a curse on my son. The juju in that village is strong," or they may say, "My sister was poisoned."

Another reason that people deny having AIDS is because the disease is linked to sexual activity. They may not want to be tested for HIV. They would rather not know if they are infected because there is no known cure. If a man's test shows that he has HIV, he knows people will say he has been running around.

---

[82] "On hearing this, Jesus said to them, 'It is not the healthy who need a doctor, but the sick. I have not come to call the righteous, but sinners'" (Mark 2:17).

If a woman's test shows she has HIV, she knows that people will say she is a bad woman. Many say that knowing their HIV status is not going to change their lifestyle, so why be tested?

Even doctors are affected by this stigma or shame attached to AIDS. Doctors must often write a death certificate for a person who has just died from AIDS. One doctor said,

> I write malaria, or TB or typhoid, but never AIDS. A death certificate can be seen by other people and the family would hate it if anyone knew.

Dr Chinua Akukwe writes,

> Although the UN estimates that 1.7 million Nigerians have died of AIDS, you will be hard pressed to identify the families of the dead as the thick wall of silence extends from hospitals that will not identify AIDS-related illness as the cause of death in death certificates; to the family members that will put out newspaper announcements that their loved one died after a "brief illness." This culture of silence extends even to the estimated 840,000 Nigerian AIDS orphans.[83]

The same could be said of many other countries. Some doctors and other health workers also fear AIDS. They may fear the reaction of the relatives if the doctor discloses that their family member has AIDS. Fear rules many of the attitudes surrounding AIDS, so the shame, secrecy and ignorance continue.

Military forces overseas

All over Africa, it is clear that the AIDS epidemic multiplies whenever military forces are sent out. Dr Anne Bayley says, "A common reaction to fear and abnormal social conditions is a

---

[83] Dr Chinue Akukwe, "AIDS in Nigeria: The Clicking Time Bomb," 2001.

breakdown in normal patterns of behaviour and an increase in sexual freedom. People see that life is short and uncertain and try to escape from their troubles by taking refuge in drink or sex. Even if a man or woman knows the risks of contracting HIV during casual sex, the risk of AIDS in five years time seems insignificant compared with the risk of death in battle tomorrow, so the lesser risk is disregarded." [84]

Nigeria has had many of its armed forces abroad for some years, especially in Liberia and Sierra Leone. Cities where there are large barracks are feeling the effects. While these soldiers were away from their homes and families, some had sexual encounters and became infected with HIV. One in nine Nigerian soldiers returned home from Sierra Leone with HIV infection. [85] Now they along with their wives and families are feeling the results of their actions. A recent report says that soldiers in many countries have HIV much more often than non-soldiers. In Tanzania, for example, 15–30 percent of soldiers were infected with HIV at a time when only eight percent of all adults were infected. Likewise 40–60 percent of Angolan soldiers were believed to be HIV infected. [86]

---

[84] Anne Bayley, *One New Humanity. The Challenge of AIDS.* SPCK International Study Guide 33, 1996.
[85] UNAIDS statistic quoted by Dr Helen Gayle, HIV/AIDS senior advisor to Bill and Melinda Gates Foundation at Prescription for Hope Conference, Washington DC, February 2002.
[86] Foreman, M. *Combat AIDS: HIV and the World's Armed Forces.* Healthlink Worldwide, 2002.

Much of Africa and the developing world have suffered civil unrest over recent years. It is likely that this has also led to more reckless sexual behaviour.

Poverty and urbanisation

Developing countries tend to be poor, and poverty worsens the HIV problem. Poverty, malnutrition and poor health care certainly worsen the HIV epidemic, though they are not the direct cause as is sometimes suggested. In fact, for many families struggling to care for sick family members who can no longer work, AIDS is the *cause* of poverty.

Dr Chinua Akukwe writes,

> Poverty in every country is the weakest spot in the war against AIDS: AIDS thrives and wallows in poverty-ridden communities.

He goes on to say Nigeria's health care system is not in a state to take on the AIDS problem.

> From the avalanche of fake drugs to the moribund healthcare infrastructure and the constant work stoppages by resident doctors, the health care system is in tatters. It is even worse at the rural areas where doctors and nurses are scarce. The UN and other multilateral institutions identify poor healthcare infrastructure as a major stumbling block to the various floating plans to supply AIDS drugs and other essential medicines to African nations. Nigeria's chronic struggles with other basic infrastructure such as road networks, water supply, sewers, sanitation, electricity, telephones, and function- ing bureaucracy complicates any potential international relief effort. The nation's much vaunted primary health care system that could have served as the backbone of a

national response to the epidemic is now on life support following successive years of neglect.[87]

What Dr Akukwe says of Nigeria is true in many other developing countries in Africa and beyond. Poverty has eaten away the defences of many families, leaving them open to HIV and all its suffering. In many large families, not all of the children can be sent to school. Families are sending many of their young people to the cities in the hope of a better life, in search of work and an income. Yet rapidly-growing, overcrowded cities can be dangerous—morally as well as physically.

Young people who move to the cities often lose the restraining influence of village life. Their parents, relations, and elders are hardly involved in their lives. No one is around to encourage them to do what is right, and no one seems to care if they do what they know is wrong. The values they once knew now seem far away and unimportant.

Young people moving to the city encounter new situations for which they are not prepared. For example, women sometimes meet men who want to buy sex from them, and men encounter women who want them to pay for sex. An employer may promise a girl a good job, but only if she has sex with him.

These young people often live in the city with a relation who has little or no time to guide them. Maybe for the first time in their lives, they have money in their pockets. With money and without guidance can come a lifestyle that involves alcohol and casual sex. Alcohol in particular leads to poor judgement and to

[87] "AIDS in Nigeria: The Clicking Time Bomb," 2001. Dr Akukwe is former Vice-Chairman of the National Council of International Health based in Washington DC.

immoral behaviour that in the light of the next day does not seem so attractive to the young person involved.

In the cities, people are watching television and videos more and more. Back home in the village there was much less of these. There may have been no electric power, and there were no video shops. The lifestyles shown in these movies look glamorous. On television and video, having many sexual partners seems to cause no serious problems. Rarely does anyone get pregnant before marriage, contract any sexually transmitted disease, or die in agony from AIDS.

Many songs on the radio talk of sexual longing. They glorify sexual pleasure-seeking and self-indulgence. When I ask young people about these songs, they say that they do not listen to the words. Perhaps they think they are not listening, but the words enter their minds nonetheless. Hour by hour, their minds are being filled by the thoughts and values of the world rather than of God. Lustful thoughts, when indulged, lead to sexual sin (James 1:13–15). There is plenty of good music for young people that gives glory to God. Let us fill our minds with music of that sort.

Many young girls come to the cities in search of work, or with a promise of work. But sometimes the job is not

> Now they are trapped....

there for them. There is no money to go back to school, and so they unwillingly become commercial sex workers. They do not want to become sex workers, but poverty, hunger and unemployment lead them to become involved with commercial sex. Sometimes it is friends who introduce them to this way of life. Once they are involved in this life, it is difficult to leave it. Now they are trapped, and even though they may know they have HIV, they do not stop having customers.

Because of poverty, parents may not have the resources to take care of their children. They sometimes push their young girls into marriage. When a marriage proposal comes, the parents may not seriously consider whether the man is suitable to marry their daughter. They may not investigate his background but are just glad to have him take responsibility for their daughter because it means one less mouth to feed in an already poor family. The girl may go into a marriage where she is abused, where the man is already in the habit of going to many different women, or where he is already infected by HIV.

For university and college students, the prospect of finishing their courses but not finding any employment is extremely depressing. In many places, poverty and unemployment are high even for graduates with good qualifications. Many degree holders find there is little work for them to do. Some have told me there is little motivation to aim high, to have ideals to live for, and to keep sex for marriage.

In some places, a man must pay a bride price before marriage. In others, a woman's family must pay a dowry to the groom or his family before she can marry. For some without a job, paying a bride price or dowry is almost impossible. Many of them feel that it is impossible to wait years to earn enough money for marriage. For them, waiting for sex inside marriage seems so far away that it is easier just to give in to temptation and have sexual partners here and there,

Separation of families

AIDS has increasingly become known in Nigeria as "The Abuja Disease." Abuja is one centre where men go to find work. More and more, I hear stories of how a husband or boyfriend has brought AIDS back from Abuja. Perhaps elsewhere AIDS is known as the Kampala disease, the Lusaka disease, the Nairobi disease and so on. In these large urban areas, many men live separated from their wives.

The issue of separation is related to poverty, migratory labour, and urbanisation. Many husbands are separated from their wives because of work. They go to a mining camp, factory, or the big city, leaving their wives in the village or town. Some of these men are professionals like civil servants, bank workers, teachers or even church workers on transfer. Others are workers such as electricians, miners, carpenters, or traders. The wives often have secure jobs that they must keep in order to have money to pay for expenses like children's school fees. Thus, they feel unable to move even when their husbands are posted away. Many wives must stay at home to farm so they can feed the family. For all these reasons and others, the husbands go alone far from home. They earn little money, so they cannot travel home often to see their wives.

With the small income these men earn in the city, they may visit commercial sex workers, many of whom have HIV. Or, maybe the man has a girlfriend in the city to ease his loneliness, a girlfriend who has already been infected. When these men go home to their village, they infect their wives.

The wives are also lonely and may be having sexual partners during their husband's absence. The partners may be schoolteachers, soldiers, police officers or government workers sent to work in the villages and towns. These men are also far from their families. So the circle of infection continues.

It is unfortunate, but teachers across Africa have a high HIV infection rate. Women sometimes need cash to pay school fees, and female students are in a tempting situation when looking for top marks. Sadly, both groups service the teachers with sex. The teachers are professionals who should know better, but like so many others, they do not think AIDS will hit them. Like so many others, they are deceived by the long period between the time a person is infected and the time symptoms appear. This stops them from seeing the connection between their behaviour and the illnesses that come many years later.

On my travels, I have given AIDS literature to many police officers and soldiers I have met at roadblocks. They sometimes say something like

- "I am far from home and from my wife."
- "I have no money to get married. And I am a man. You don't expect me to do without sex!"
- "Sex is natural. It is not like drinking beer or smoking cigarettes. I cannot stop sex. And anyway, I will die someday anyway, so I should have as much fun as I can before then!"

Travel

Many people travel away from home for long periods. Long distance lorry drivers and traders are carrying the virus all over the world. They do not necessarily have more sex partners, but the partners may be spread over the whole country or to other countries. Many "lorry stops" where drivers stop to rest have girls offering sex. Sometimes people say that as the mosquito spreads malaria, so the lorry driver is the "mosquito" that carries AIDS.

Lorry drivers, however, are only *one* type of "mosquito" spreading HIV. When businessmen or government officials travel away from home for conferences and workshops, there are often many girls around the hotels ready to supply them with easy sex. Sometimes the host of an event may even supply girls for his guests. These girls have already been infected by other clients and will pass the infection on to these "big men," who will carry it home to their wives.

Recently, a counsellor asked an HIV-infected man whether he had been faithful to his wife. He said he had. The counsellor went on to ask more questions, trying to learn where the virus had come from. Yet he could not find many clues. The counsellor then asked directly, "Have you ever had sex with anyone apart from your wife?" This time, the man answered yes.

The man explained that when he travelled on business, his boss provided "hospitality" for him where he stayed. However, he did not look on having this sex as being unfaithful to his wife. It was just hospitality! I wonder whether such girls know what a risk they are taking. Tragically, if they are young girls in the home of the man providing hospitality, they may have no choice.

Traditional practices

Polygamy: A state medical officer in charge of HIV/AIDS prevention lamented how rapidly AIDS is spreading in his state, especially through polygamous marriages. When the virus enters a polygamous family, it will affect many people. After the death of a polygamous husband and after the mourning period has passed, the wives may marry into other polygamous families, and many more people quickly become infected.

Bride price: One familiar custom in much of Africa is the high cost of a wedding, due, in part, to the large bride price or dowry. Many young men *want* to marry, but cannot afford it. The girl's family traditionally asks for several cows or much money, sometimes more than a man can earn in a year, especially if the girl is well educated. The young men cannot meet such families' demands. They find marriage financially impossible for many years. So instead of marrying to satisfy their natural sexual desires, as the apostle Paul teaches us in the book of First Corinthians, they fall into sexual temptation and sin.

One young man recently said to me, "I am 30 years old. I am still trying to gather together money for a bride price, so I can't afford to marry. Do you not think I have done well by only having sex with three different girls up to now?" What can the church do in this area? Can we address this problem as a way of combating AIDS?

An excessive bride price can also cause families and prospective husbands to view women as property or slaves. Some fathers sell their daughters to the highest bidder. The husbands then see their wives as their own property, to do with just as they please.

> Pastor Wilberforce Owori of the Frontline AIDS Support Network in Tororo [Uganda], recounted how he counseled a young man who beat his wife into a coma because she asked about his having sex with other women who might have HIV. He recalled: "Men don't want women to mention if they are going out with women with HIV. Women have no authority. They are

treated as property. He has paid the dowry [bride price], she is in his home."[88]

Sharing wives: Wife hospitality (allowing a guest in your home to have sexual relations with your wife) and widow inheritance (where a brother marries or has sex with his dead brother's wife) also increase the spread of HIV. Widow inheritance originally served as a way to provide for the family of the dead husband. It is often abused now, however, to the extent that the husband's brothers may force the widow into sex or into a marriage she does not want. Women are often powerless to refuse because of they have no property rights and no economic power to survive on their own. Frequently, they do not even have the right to keep their own children. In all these ways they are treated as little more than slaves or property, unable to refuse dangerous or undesirable marriages.[89]

Sex on ritual occasions: People in many cultures make sex a part of certain rituals. For example, in some places funerals (burials) may be a time when drunkenness and sex are widely practised, and women may be given to men for sex. In other places, there are festivals or celebrations when people are expected to have sex with others besides their spouses, or where they are free to do so if they want. The same state health officer who complained about polygamy and HIV also said that in some rural areas there are traditional festivals where sexual license is given for a few days, and that these are contributing to the fast spread of AIDS.

Some Christians say that because these occasions are part of the culture, they are acceptable. However, the Bible is quite clear

---

[88] Karanja, L. Just Die Quietly: Domestic Violence and Women's Vulnerability to HIV in Uganda. *Human Rights Watch* 15(15 (A)), 2003.

[89] Karanja, L. Just Die Quietly: Domestic Violence and Women's Vulnerability to HIV in Uganda. *Human Rights Watch* 15(15 (A)), 2003.

that such practices are an abomination to God! They were part of the pagan cultures around Israel and later around the early Christians. God condemned those practices. For example, some of the Christians at Corinth thought it was fine to have sex with the temple prostitutes. After all, it was part of the culture! In 1 Corinthians 6, however, Paul told them quite plainly that this was evil and actually harmful to their physical bodies. We belong first to God, not to this world or our culture.

Unsafe cutting: People may circumcise their sons and make tribal markings with little regard to whether the knives or blades are sterile. Even some health clinics do not take care to use new blades for circumcising baby boys. Female circumcision carries the same risk.[90] The risk of HIV is only present when a new blade is not used for each person. The virus is easily passed from one person to another on a blade with blood on it. Some cult initiation ceremonies include mixing of blood between two or more people. Of course, these can also pass on HIV.

Inferior status of women

Many HIV-infected African women received the virus from their husbands. Often women do not have the rights or status to be able to say no to sex, even when they know their husbands are having sex with other women. Husbands may know they are putting their wives at risk by having sex with other women. Yet they often refuse even to use condoms, which would give their wives *some* protection, however imperfect. If a woman questions her husband's sexual activities, he may beat her and force her to have sex. Women usually just quietly accept their husband's unfaithfulness, not because they want to, but because

---

[90] Female circumcision is a dangerous procedure that causes immense suffering for women, stops them from enjoying sexual pleasure in marriage and creates difficulties for both mother and baby during childbirth. The practice is often called "female genital mutilation."

they have no power to do otherwise. A friend of mine whose husband was going out for sex told me, "All I can do is pray." Others say, "What can I do? He is a man." The church needs to do much teaching in this area.

After infection with HIV, a woman may develop AIDS and die before her husband. This does not necessarily mean that she was infected before her husband. It may be because her health and nutrition are not as good as her husband's. Her body pays the price of repeated pregnancies, manual work, and eating less meat or other nutritious foods than her husband does. Meanwhile, her husband does less manual work, eats meat away from home, and does not have to bother with the stress of pregnancies. Gossipers and onlookers often point their fingers at the wife. They say she must be the one who brought HIV into the family as she is the one who is ill, while her husband is still healthy.

> ... there was only "small HIV" in his blood....

Men who are widowed when their wife dies from AIDS sometimes marry again and infect their second wife before they become ill and die from AIDS. Recently one man whose wife had died from AIDS was preparing to marry. He declared to his friends that he had gone for an HIV test and that there was only "small HIV" in his blood and it was not bothering him. This man is deceiving himself and the woman he wants to marry. "Small HIV" means that he too will die from AIDS and will likely take his second wife with him.

Another sign of the inferior status of women is rape. Rape can pass on HIV, especially because of the violent trauma that tears mucous membranes. This opens the door for HIV infection. Child rape may be especially common in South Africa. Some experts say this is because of the common false belief that sex with a virgin can cure AIDS. Others doubt this explanation and feel the more important causes are a culture of violence, the low status of women, and that rapists are often not punished.[91]

Over the last twenty years, many have discussed and debated the reasons for the spreading epidemic of HIV. Though not all the reasons are clear, it *is* clear that we are still in the early days of the epidemic. Many more millions are going to die. Without significant behaviour change, without an outpouring of prayer and repentance, and without involvement of the people of Jesus Christ in all levels of society, we will not see significant improvement for years to come.

Discussion Questions

1. What do you think are some of the values of your community or church that contribute to the spread of AIDS?

2. What are some traditions of marriage and divorce that promote the spread of AIDS? Using Biblical teaching, what can you do to change those traditions?

3. What cultural practices in your area contribute to the spread of AIDS? What can you do to change them?

4. Discuss how you can prevent the young girls in your own family, who are at highest risk of HIV infection, from being infected.

5. What can the church teach and do to give women more protection from AIDS?

6. What can the church do to help make women safer from rape and sexual violence? (Do not forget to think of how the church should address the men's role.)

---

[91] Jewkes, R., L. Martin, *et al.*, The Virgin Cleansing Myth: Cases of Child Rape Are Not Exotic. *Lancet* 359(9307): 711, 2002.

Ibrahim's behaviour destroyed his chance of a happy family life

Ibrahim and his family[92]

Ibrahim left school when he was 17. He married Aisha soon afterwards, but only because he had made her pregnant. He had little choice once Aisha's father learned that she was pregnant. Ibrahim and Aisha had a son, Daniel, and then a daughter inside two years. Ibrahim thought that he did love Aisha, but there was no work to keep food for them all, especially now with the new baby. There was nothing else for Ibrahim to do but to leave home and try to find work, so he went to live with an uncle in the capital. He did some small trading there and tried to get work building houses.

[92] The idea for this story is from Dr Bob Whittacker, Nigerian Christian Hospital, Abia State, Nigeria.

His wife and children still lived in the village. Ibrahim did not go home often because he was so busy with his building work. However, he did try to go home about three times a year to see his family and friends.

In December, Ibrahim was going home to his village. The year had been bad for him. The building trade had been poor. The economy was down and business was not moving. Things had been hard. As a result, Ibrahim had not been able to get home to see his family in the village for a long time. Now he was riding on the back of a lorry rather than in the luxury bus. In his bag he had a few gifts for the family.

As he travelled, he thought on things back in the capital. Though Ibrahim had been away from his wife Aisha for a long time, he had not been entirely alone in the capital. He had a girl friend called Amina. She was a comfort to him when things went badly. He had come to depend on her. Amina liked to buy costly things, but Ibrahim's salary had not been good for that. Amina had other men friends. Ibrahim used to quarrel with her over that, but Amina was a stubborn woman. Ibrahim was in love with Amina and could not bear to quarrel with her for long. Amina was seeing another man who had a car, a white Mercedes. He dared not ask her about it. What should he do?

"Father, Father," a little voice came from below. Ibrahim looked down from the lorry and saw his little 4-year-old son Daniel running alongside, grinning and waving. The lorry stopped and Ibrahim jumped down and pulled his son into his arms. Daniel's little friends, too, were shouting with excitement. Ibrahim trekked happily to his home. His wife did not come out to greet him. Some friends stopped to greet him. "Where is your Mother?" Ibrahim asked Daniel in a quiet moment.

"Oh, she has taken the baby to the clinic. The baby is not well. She has fever." Ibrahim told Daniel to stay at home and he set off for the clinic. As he turned out of the compound, Aisha appeared on the road. She was carrying the sick baby on her back. She approached quietly and greeted her husband. She looked older somehow, and her clothes were dull. Ibrahim thought of Amina and her bright clothes and nice perfume. He took the child and carried her into the house.

Later that evening, Aisha spoke to him plainly. "Husband, life here has been hard while you have been away. You have sent money only twice."

"I know, my dear," said Ibrahim, "but things have been hard for me also. Business has been bad. There has been little work. I myself have had to struggle."

"Anyway, now that you are here you can help us," Aisha said. "The clinic nurse says we must take our child to hospital for a test. She thinks her blood is weak."

"Well," said Ibrahim, "I can take her there tomorrow. We can buy whatever medicine the doctor prescribes. Do not be discouraged, wife. There is no problem. I have brought a few gifts for you and the children. But let me first go and greet my brothers."

Ibrahim went down to the village and passed the place where the men were drinking. He did not mean to stay, but of course he stopped to greet all his friends. There were rounds of drinks, and Ibrahim spent some time talking to everyone.

"What do you think about this AIDS that we are hearing about?" said one friend. "I was listening to the radio, and they said that this AIDS is carried back from the big cities to the villages during the holidays."

"Oh, I do not believe any of it," said Ibrahim. "I think that it is not true. People are only trying to frighten us. I have never seen anyone with this sickness. I think it is an invention of the white people to worry the black people. In the capital, they say that AIDS means the American Invention to Discourage Sex." All Ibrahim's friends laughed much at that and passed round more local beer.

American Invention to Discourage Sex?

"Well, I have heard that mosquitoes can give you AIDS," another said. "If a mosquito bites you, you can get AIDS. I don't know if it's true."

"The government should collect everyone with AIDS and lock them up so they cannot spread the thing," said another. "Yes," shouted everybody, "we do not want these people here. Get rid of them. They are dirtying the whole place. If anyone in this village brings this sickness, we should drive them out. If they die here, their body should not be buried nearby." And so they continued talking into the night. When Ibrahim came home, Aisha was in bed. She appeared to be sleeping.

The next morning, Ibrahim took tea. He had a headache. His wife reminded him about the child. Ibrahim bathed, then carried the child to hospital. The laboratory test showed that the child indeed had weak blood. The doctor ordered a blood transfusion, and Ibrahim gave his own blood for his child. The hospital did not test his blood for HIV before transfusing it into his daughter. Ibrahim felt happy that he had helped his daughter. The child stayed for four days in the hospital, and then returned home looking better.

The Christmas season passed, but Ibrahim did not feel well. He often had headache and began to have body pains and diarrhoea. He went to the village pharmacy. The man there gave him two injections at the back of the shop. After injecting Ibrahim, the man washed out the needle and syringe with water from a tap. He then used the same needle to give chloroquine to the girl who came after Ibrahim. Ibrahim also had itchy rashes over his body, and the pharmacy worker gave him some cream that helped somewhat. Christmas was not happy for the family, and Ibrahim wanted to get back to the capital. Even though he did have sex with Aisha several times, she seemed little fun, and there seemed to be little life in the house.

Ibrahim returned to the capital the second week of January. Another Christmas and New Year were finished. However, things were not entirely as they appeared.

What Ibrahim, his friends, Aisha, and you and I did not know was that Ibrahim was infected with HIV. He had received the virus from Amina, who had received it from the man with the white Mercedes, who probably had received it from one of his other girlfriends. Several people were infected because of Ibrahim's behaviour.

Ibrahim remained in the capital and continued to see Amina. However, after two years Amina became sick and could not get well. She spent much money going to doctors, and Ibrahim was most concerned. She kept having diarrhoea and was terribly thin. Eventually, she left the capital to go back to her village. She decided to try herbal medicine in the village, but it did not help. She died after six months of sickness.

At about the same time, Ibrahim travelled home to his village. He was shocked to find his daughter seriously ill. Ibrahim remembered giving his blood to his little daughter but thought nothing of it. She was rushed off to hospital, but despite all efforts of the doctors, the child died. The doctors said that it was a strange illness, like a germ in the blood, but did not tell Ibrahim exactly what was wrong. "Maybe it is witchcraft," Ibrahim thought.

Not long after, Ibrahim began to have fever and cough. He also had pain when passing urine and had a large, painless ulcer on his genital area. He just could not find the right medicine. The cough continued for six months while Ibrahim became thinner. Every night, he slept little because the cough kept him awake.

He went to the best hospital, where the doctor did a thorough examination and ordered three sputum tests one after the other. He also sent Ibrahim for a chest x-ray. The sputum tests were positive and the doctor told Ibrahim he had tuberculosis. The doctor ordered blood tests. They showed that Ibrahim had a sexually transmitted disease, syphilis, and HIV. Ibrahim died the following year, followed soon after by his wife Aisha. Little Daniel was an orphan.

There was no schooling for little Daniel. Food was scarce, so Daniel was not well nourished. When Daniel was sick, his grandparents could not afford medicine. Today Daniel is having a difficult life. The behaviour of his father far away in the capital has had long-lasting results.

Discussion Questions

1. How many people were infected with HIV as a result of Ibrahim's behaviour? How was each of them infected?

2. What do you see as the root cause of all the suffering in Ibrahim's family? Is there any way the local church could have helped deal with the root cause?

3. If Ibrahim's wife had known about her husband's life and girlfriend in the capital, could she have changed the situation? Or, was she powerless to protect herself and her family? If she was powerless, how could the Christian message and the actions of the local church help women like her?

4. Discuss the idea that Ibrahim's friends suggested, locking up everyone with AIDS. Is this a Christian response? Do you think it would help solve the AIDS problem? Why or why not?

Chapter Ten
False Beliefs and Practices about Sex and Childbearing

Every culture has its own beliefs and practices about the process of generating new life. Africans, of all people, appreciate and guard the sacred value of conceiving and bearing children. Many of our beliefs and practices probably began as the community searched for ways to protect and preserve families and new life. Take, for example, the idea that a breast-feeding mother should not have sex. This might have started as a way to ensure that the baby grew old enough to survive, before being displaced by a new baby.

Although these customs doubtless came from good intentions, some are based on misunderstanding and ignorance. In the past, the traditions may have helped the community survive. Now, in our changed world, some of the same customs are leading to suffering or death.

Many traditional customs and beliefs are still good and helpful indeed. An example is that African mothers breast-feed their children for a long time. Many Western countries are still struggling to teach their mothers the importance of breast-feeding, while Africans have preserved that good custom.

Now, let us discuss some of the harmful African traditions related to sex and childbearing. Some are found only in certain areas, while others are more common. Proper understanding of these matters will lead to healthier family relationships and can help limit sex before marriage and outside marriage. Ignorance and false beliefs are causing AIDS to spread, while true understanding will help prevent that spread.

Myth: No sex while breast-feeding the baby

Some people believe that if there is sex during the time a woman is breast-feeding, the husband's semen will poison his wife's breast milk and injure the baby. Some believe that the baby will look unhealthy and malnourished. Some say the baby will have eye infections that will attract flies. Sometimes, older relations will scold a young mother if the baby has eye infections, or is weak. They tell her that it is her fault for having sex with her husband while continuing to breast-feed. Because of these fears, quarrelling and bad relationships occur inside the marriage. When the wife refuses sex, her husband may feel justified going elsewhere for sex. He may bring home a sexually transmitted disease, possibly the AIDS virus.

There is *no* reason for the couple to avoid sex when the baby is breast-feeding. The sperm and semen do not enter the woman's blood. They certainly do not reach the breast milk. They enter only the vagina and the womb and do not go near the breast milk. During the first six weeks or so after the baby's birth, sexual activity may be painful for the mother. Beyond that, the husband and wife should continue enjoying sex together as God intended.

It is best for the mother not to become pregnant for at least two years from her last pregnancy. This allows her to recover her strength fully and to breast-feed and care for her baby well. If the couple do not want another pregnancy soon, they can learn how to space their children. Their doctor, clinic, or family planning centre can help them learn the best child spacing methods, given their own circumstances. Sex in marriage is God's gift and should be enjoyed.

Myth: No sex after menopause

Another false belief is that there should be no sex after menopause, that is, after the menses or monthly period stops completely. Many people see it as a shame for the woman to allow sex after menopause. Some believe that sex after the menopause will cause lumps (fibroids) in the womb. These false beliefs often cause conflict in a marriage and may push the husband to have sex with other women.

Sexual desire and enjoyment do not stop at menopause, and there is no reason to avoid sex then. Fibroids or other lumps have no relation to sex. Intercourse may sometimes be uncomfortable since the vagina can be drier than in earlier life, but a bit of lubricant like KY Jelly before intercourse can solve that problem. Most pharmacies sell these lubricants. Sex should continue to be an enjoyable part of the bond between husband and wife after menopause.

Myth: If there is no male child, the wife is to blame

Another false belief is that it is the fault of the wife when she does not produce a male child. This is unfair. Whether the baby is a boy or a girl depends on the husband's sperm and is not the "fault" of the wife. Therefore, if "fault" is to be given, it is the husband who decides the baby's gender. Sometimes, if a woman does not bear a son, the husband may bring in a second wife to produce one, or may go outside the marriage. This can bring AIDS into the family. Sometimes, men seek to marry the daughter of a woman who produces many sons and a few daughters. They think that such a wife will be sure to produce many sons. We repeat, whether a baby is a boy or a girl is decided by the husband's sperm and has nothing to do with the woman. Also, having a boy or a girl does not depend on the strength of the husband's blood. The husband's sperm alone decides it.[93]

Myth: No sex during pregnancy

Some think that sex between husband and wife during pregnancy is wrong. Some say the husband's semen will cover

the baby, the baby will smell, the baby will be harmed, and the eyes will be affected. They also say the baby will be jaundiced, with yellowed eyes. Older relatives may scold a woman if there is jaundice, saying the wife should not have allowed her husband near her when she was pregnant. None of this is true.

The myth of no sex during pregnancy and breast-feeding means that the husband often has to go many months without sex. Some husbands use this as an

---

[93] The man's sperm and woman's egg join at conception. Each carries one "sex chromosome." The egg always carries an X chromosome. The sperm can bring either another X chromosome or a Y. If the sperm brings an X, the child will be a girl. If the sperm brings a Y, the child will be a boy. The man's sperm, not the woman's egg, determines the sex of the baby.

excuse to go elsewhere for sex. It is sometimes even accepted that the husband, without blame, can find partners elsewhere while his wife is pregnant. Thus, the false myth of "no sex during pregnancy" contributes to the spread of HIV.

There is no reason why a husband and wife should avoid sex during pregnancy, except perhaps during the last month before delivery when it can be uncomfortable for the woman. God has designed the womb and the baby's membranes to provide excellent protection against everything from the outside world. The husband's semen cannot touch or harm the baby in any way.

The white covering on the baby's skin at birth is called *vernix caseosa* or simply vernix. It is God's way of protecting the baby's skin. It should be found on every healthy newborn baby. Neither vernix nor jaundice has anything to do with sex during pregnancy.

Myth: Repeated miscarriages are due to having sex with various men

In some areas, people say that if a woman has repeated miscarriages, the cause is "mixed sperm," meaning that she has been with men other than her husband. This is medically and scientifically false. Some men use this false belief as an excuse for going out after other women, thus bringing home HIV and AIDS.

Myth: No sexual intercourse for a long time after a stillbirth

Some believe that if a woman delivers a dead baby (stillbirth), her husband should not have intercourse with her for at least one and a half years. They believe that it will take this time before the womb is ready for another baby. There is no medical reason for this. About six weeks after the stillbirth, sexual relationships can resume. However, it is best to use a child-spacing method so that the woman's body will have time to build up its strength for another pregnancy. Child-spacing after any pregnancy is important, whether or not the baby was born alive.

Myth: Women should not show evidence of enjoying sexual intercourse

Many people believe and proclaim that a woman should not enjoy sex. They think it shameful for her to enjoy sexual relationships with her husband. They say that she should pretend she does not enjoy it. Her older relatives sometimes teach her that she should "fight off" the husband and not agree to sexual relationships more than twice in a week. They tell her that she should certainly never ask for sex or show affection to her husband lest he take advantage of her.

Because of this belief, many women drive their husbands out of the house to commercial sex workers, who enjoy (or pretend to enjoy) sex and act very differently from the way their wives act. Though the men themselves are responsible before God for their sinful behaviour, the wives have, unknowingly, contributed to the temptation.

Paul teaches clearly the truth about this matter in I Corinthians 7.[94] The wife and husband have equal rights to ask for sex in

---

94 "But because there is so much sexual immorality, each man should have his own wife, and each woman should have her own husband. The husband should not deprive his wife of sexual intimacy, which is her right as a married woman, nor should the wife deprive her husband. The wife gives authority over her body to her husband, and the husband also gives authority over his body to his wife. So do not deprive each other of sexual relations. The only exception to this rule would be the agreement of both husband and wife to refrain from sexual intimacy for a limited time, so they can give themselves more completely to prayer." 1 Cor 7:2–5, NLT.

marriage. A wife should feel free to be the one who suggests that they have sex together. Neither husband nor wife should "deprive" the other. Both husband and wife should try hard to please each other sexually as in other ways. Showing love in this way will certainly reduce the risk of immorality and HIV.

Myth: No sex makes a man weak in his body

"Thank you for your talk, Teacher. It has really made me think. But I have a question. I have heard people say that if a man does not have sex often, he will become weak and sick. Some of my friends say that if I don't have enough sex, I will not develop properly, emotionally or physically. Is that true?"

Sometimes young men ask me questions like this. The ideas they have heard are false and harmful. The very opposite is true.

Young men and women who avoid sex before marriage often progress more quickly in school and university and make better progress in every way compared to their promiscuous friends. Many young men are filled with groundless fears on this issue. This is a selfish idea about sex. Would God have told us to abstain from sex outside marriage if it were bad for our health?

Sometimes, after marriage, the husband and wife will be separated for a time. Again there is no reason for the man to feel that he will become sick without sex. The joy will be greater when he and his wife come together again. At the same time, husband and wife should remember God's teaching that they should not stay apart sexually for a long time.

Myth: Sex with a virgin will cure me from AIDS

Some HIV-infected men falsely think that having sex with a virgin will cure them. In this way, they are likely to infect young girls. They may rape them looking for a cure. This belief may be more widespread in South Africa than in East and West Africa. Of course, the belief is completely untrue.

Myth: Women who do not conceive are cursed by their ancestors

Some people believe that a woman unable to produce children is cursed by her ancestors. This myth can lead to more sex outside marriage. Sometimes, childless women may use various rituals and sacrifices to try to remove the curses that they believe to be the cause. The truth is that either the husband *or* the wife may have a medical problem that blocks conception. Sometimes, though not always, good medical advice and treatment can help childless couples to conceive. Childlessness may be used as an excuse for sexual activity outside of the marriage, leading to HIV and other sexually transmitted infections.[95]

Discussion Questions

1. Do you or people around you believe any of the myths listed? Which ones? What reasons do you or others have for the beliefs?

2. Are there any other myths or false beliefs not mentioned here that promote the spread of AIDS?

3. Do any of these myths consciously or unconsciously affect your own behaviour? Are you willing to change your behaviour after reading this chapter?

---

[95] Some of the ideas for this chapter come from Dr Leonie McSweeney, *A Challenge to Love...Changing Behaviour*. Ibadan. Ambassador Productions.

Chapter Eleven
Is There Any Vaccine Or Cure For AIDS?

There is no known cure or vaccine for AIDS despite many years of research into this complex illness. Researchers have been trying to find a vaccine against the disease and to find drugs to kill the virus. Advances have been painfully slow. Although there is not cure yet, there are medicines that can fight the virus (Chapter Twelve), and others that treat the opportunistic illnesses that come with HIV. These can often prolong life and improve health.

What is a vaccine?

A vaccine is a special material that "teaches" the body's immune system how to fight against a certain disease. The white cells, soldiers of the immune system, can learn to fight the virus only after they have *"seen"* it in the body. Take measles for example. What happens the first time measles virus enters your body? If you have not had measles vaccine, the virus will multiply and cause illness. But in a few days, your white blood cells learn to fight the virus, and you recover. Those cells have good memory and will remember at once how to fight measles virus if it enters the body again. The same cells, though, would not know how to fight a different virus such as yellow fever.

Measles vaccine contains a weak form of measles virus. When it is injected into the body, it is too weak to cause sickness. The white cells recognise the weak measles virus as an enemy, however, and learn to fight it. Later, when the real virus enters the body, the cells are already trained and fully prepared to fight it off before it can cause sickness.

Is there an HIV vaccine?

As soon as HIV was discovered, scientists began thinking about how to develop a vaccine. Attempts to develop vaccines began more than ten years ago, but to date they have all failed, mainly due to the ability of the virus to *mutate* or change its shape. There have been many reports and stories of vaccines being tested, but none have reached the point of being safe and effective.

Scientists are still trying hard to develop vaccines. The human trials are still in the early stages. So far, they have concentrated on seeing whether a given vaccine is safe—the biggest fear being that it could accidentally trigger HIV.

Scientists are testing anti-HIV vaccines in several countries. These trials are all difficult for many reasons, a few of which are these:

- HIV can hide from the immune system. Even if the white cells learn to fight it, some of the virus hides away.
- There is no kind of animal that is good for testing a vaccine. Only humans get sick from HIV, so scientists cannot simply test a new vaccine on rats, monkeys, or other animals.
- HIV works differently from any human virus we have known before. Because of the differences, a weakened form of the virus would not be safe.
- HIV has many different strains or types. Different types are more common in different countries. A vaccine against one type may not protect against another type.
- Scientists are finding that the immune system is more complicated than we thought it was. There is still much that is not understood about how the body might protect itself from HIV. This makes it hard to know how to create a vaccine.[96]

Scientists are working hard to find a good vaccine. As of 2004, there are at least 39 vaccines being tested somewhere, nearly all on a small scale. Many of the vaccines now being tested are developed specifically for HIV strains that are common in western countries, rather than those found in Africa. There is progress but it is slow. The president of the International AIDS Vaccine Initiative has said we should not expect an effective vaccine before the year 2009.[97]

Scientists are convinced that for the long-term war on HIV, vaccines are the way forward. Economic arguments are now driving research as well. While the initial cost of developing vaccines may be high, it is minimal when compared to the proj-

---

[96] Stine, G. J., *AIDS Update 2003*. Prentice Hall, New Jersey, 2003.
[97] Seth Berkley quoted in Reuters news report, 19 June 2003.

ected costs of using drugs to treat the virus and its symptoms in the world's estimated 42 million HIV infected people.

Unproven and questionable cures

There are many "quack" doctors and healers of every kind who claim to cure AIDS (for a fee!). Some of their treatments may appear temporarily to improve the life of the person living with HIV/AIDS. This might be because of added antiretroviral drugs, antibiotics, anti-HIV substances in plants, psychological effects, or for other unknown reasons. Even if such treatments do *help* people with HIV, none of them actually cures HIV.

There is still no cure for HIV/AIDS. Often when a person feels better after some of these costly treatments, he believes that he is cured. He is not. People must be encouraged not to use all their resources running after questionable cures. However, if simple remedies that relieve symptoms can be found, we should encourage these to be used.

Prayer for healing

As Christians, we believe God can cure anyone from AIDS. Prayer for healing and daily strength should be part of our ministry to those with AIDS. A God who can raise the dead is able to heal if he wishes. For reasons known only to God, he does not often bring healing, and those claiming healing should have blood tests carried out to confirm that healing.

Discussion Question

1. If your family member wanted to spend a lot of money on a so-called cure for AIDS from a traditional doctor or any other source, what advice would you give him or her? Why would you give this advice?

Chapter Twelve
Antiretroviral Drugs

We have continued to remind you there is no cure for HIV. A cure would have to be something that would completely rid the body of the virus, ending it one hundred percent. Thousands of scientists and doctors around the world are working hard to find a cure, but until now there is none. Most scientists do not think a cure will be found in the next ten years. Certainly, if a true cure is discovered, news of it will quickly spread around the world.

If there is no cure, what are the antiretroviral drugs (anti-HIV drugs or *ARVs*) that everyone is talking of? Are they not cures? Unfortunately, no. In this chapter, we will look at what these drugs *can* do and what they *cannot* do. We will also see some of their advantages and some of their problems.

A little history

AIDS was first officially recognised as a disease in 1981, but the cause was not known. It was two years later, in 1983, that scientists discovered the virus, HIV, as the cause. No one knew which drugs might be able to fight the virus. The first successful drug was *zidovudine* (ZDV, AZT or Retrovir). It was approved in the United States as an anti-HIV drug in 1987. It was extremely costly and caused problems such as anaemia (lack of red blood cells) in some people. Also, it helped only somewhat and only for a time.

Since 1987, many new drugs have proven successful against HIV. Some are closely related to zidovudine, while others are completely different. Even though companies discovered many drugs, one could scarcely find those drugs in Africa or other parts of the developing world before the year 2000 because of their great cost. Drug companies wanted to make a good profit on these treatments.

In the past few years, though, things have changed. Drug companies in developed countries are beginning to supply antiretroviral drugs to poorer countries at low cost. Also, they are agreeing to allow some countries of the developing world to produce the drugs themselves. One of the big reasons for the change is that Christians (and others) in Africa, North America, and elsewhere have pointed to God's demand that people and countries treat each other with justice and fairness.

Now, ARVs (antiretrovirals) are becoming more available in Africa and elsewhere. This is cause for rejoicing, but as we shall see, these drugs are not the answer to the epidemic of HIV. Let us look further into how the drugs work and what we can expect of them.

Basic points about antiretroviral drugs

ARVs stop the virus from multiplying

We call these drugs "antiretroviral" because HIV is a retrovirus. So in effect "antiretroviral" means "anti-HIV." We will call them ARV for short. These drugs do not kill the virus. At best, they only stop it from multiplying in the body to produce more virus. But some of the virus is always hiding and ready to multiply when it can.[98] It can hide, sleeping deep in the body, until one day it awakes and begins to multiply and cause illness again. While it is hidden and sleeping, no drugs can touch it.

Antiretroviral drugs are like locks on a prison door. They make prisoners of the virus but do not kill them. As long as they are in place and strong, the prisoners must remain in their cells. But if the locks become weak or spoiled the prisoners will escape. Likewise the drugs keep the virus "asleep" or in prison, but it is always ready to awaken and escape. If one stops taking the drugs, the infection returns.

---

[98] Even when ARVs are being used successfully, a small amount of the virus is multiplying.

It should be clear now why ARVs do not cure AIDS or HIV infection. The only way to cure the disease would be to kill all the virus, or make it permanently unable to multiply. The drugs cannot do this because of the way they work and the way the virus hides. This is why one must continue taking the drugs the rest of one's life, trying to keep the virus "in prison" or "asleep."[99]

ARVs can slow the illness of AIDS

The good news is, even though ARV drugs cannot cure HIV, they can help keep people with HIV healthy and free from the symptoms of AIDS. As long as most of the virus is kept "asleep," the body's immune system can keep up its defences. When the immune system is working, the person is less likely to get illnesses such as tuberculosis, diarrhoea, and pneumonia. He or she is more likely to remain strong and able to work and to take care of the family. For this reason, ARV drugs can be helpful indeed. *If* treatment is successful and the virus does not overcome it (see below), someone can live for many, many years without AIDS, though the virus is still in the body.

ARVs do not prevent transmission of HIV

Antiretroviral drugs do not stop the spread of HIV through sex!

It is most important to understand that the person taking ARVs can still pass on the virus through sex or by the blood. In fact, one of the concerns about widespread use of ARVs is that HIV may actually spread faster if

---

[99] In some cases it might be acceptable to "interrupt" the treatment, stopping it for a time, but only with the advice of a doctor who is expert at treating HIV/AIDS.

people become falsely reassured that they will not pass on or receive HIV from sexual intercourse. ARVs do not make sex "safe."

ARVs do not work forever: the problem of resistance

The bad news is that ARVs cannot usually keep the virus in prison forever. HIV is clever and mischievous. It is constantly trying to find ways to wake up and escape from the "prison" of the drug. It is as if the virus is trying to find the right key for the lock on the prison door. Once it finds the key, the lock is useless and the virus escapes. In other words, the virus finds a way to "escape" from the effect of the drug. This is called "resistance," because the virus can now resist the drug. Resistance is bad, of course, because it means that the drug is now less useful (or even useless) for the person. Even worse, someone with a resistant virus might pass it on to someone else. When that happens, the drug will be of little use to that other person.

Preventing resistance

You can see it is important to try to prevent or delay resistance. That is, we must stop the virus from discovering the key to the prison. How can we do this?

Take Every Dose

One way to prevent resistance is to take every dose and take it at the right time. Most people find it hard to take medicines regularly. It is easy to forget, especially when we must take the medicine more than once or twice daily. We may be away from home and not have the tablets with us. We may be in the midst of work or a meeting and we do not want to stop to take medicine. We may feel well and think that we do not need the medicine today. We may forget to collect more medicine before our supply finishes, or we have no money, or the distance to the clinic is too great. Perhaps the medicine makes us feel ill, or causes a headache. There are so many other reasons that make it difficult to always take the medicine.

It is easy to understand why we may miss taking the drugs. Sadly, the virus does not care about the reason, and it does not forgive. It begins to wake up as the drug disappears from the body. It begins multiplying and searching for the key to the lock. It may not find the key at once, so the drug may remain effective. But the more times we miss or delay taking the drug for any reason, the more likely the virus will find the key and escape permanently from that drug. To make matters worse, the virus will also be able to escape from other similar drugs.

Drug Combinations

Another way to help solve the resistance problem is to use a combination of drugs rather than a single drug alone. Suppose you are taking two drugs that are effective against the HIV in your body. This is like having two different locks on the prison door. Even if some of the virus discovers the key to one lock, it cannot escape because the second lock is still in place. Because ARVs are not perfect locks, we need to use at least three of them in most cases.

This point is important and you should understand it well. It is better to have no locks on the prison doors for a time than to have only one or two! If there is only one, then the virus will find the key and that lock will be permanently useless. With two locks, the risk is less but still unacceptable. People who take only one or two of the drugs may find that they have become useless, and the illness will worsen.[100]

---

[100] What if the person is already sick with AIDS, needs drugs, but cannot obtain or afford all three drugs? Taking one or two may help him for a time. However he will probably develop resistance before long and may even pass it on to others. This is why international groups

For this reason, treatment begins with three drugs. It is never advisable to take only a single drug of those widely available in Africa, because resistance will develop quickly. Fortunately, two or three drugs are often combined into a single tablet. For example, one of the most common ARV tablets is Combivir, a combination of the two drugs zidovudine and lamivudine. A person taking Combivir is actually taking a combination of two drugs. There are also tablets such as Triommune and Trizivir that include three drugs, so someone may need to take only this one kind of tablet. Combining drugs into one tablet is more convenient for the patient. Equally important, it ensures that the drugs will be taken together so the virus will always be behind three locks.

Things to consider before starting antiretroviral treatment

Whether to start antiretroviral therapy and when to start are important decisions not to be taken lightly. The decision is rarely urgent, and we know that the drugs will be most helpful in people who have considered well and carefully before starting treatment. Remember, there is no end to taking the drugs. Once someone begins ARVs, they will need to continue taking the drugs the rest of their lives (or until the drugs become useless or too harmful).[101]

It is important to see that the question is not whether to *care* for the person with HIV, but whether to use antiretroviral drugs and when to start them. Delaying ARV treatment is not the same as

---

like WHO and Global Fund are trying to ensure that everyone on antiretroviral therapy will have continuing good access to *all* the drugs.

[101] Doctors are still investigating the question of whether people can stop taking their antiretroviral drugs for a time in certain situations. Until now the answer is not clear. Certainly the drugs should not be stopped except under the care of an expert HIV physician and with the availability of advanced laboratory tests including CD4 count and viral load.

doing nothing (see story on page 244). Both before and during treatment with ARVs, other parts of care are important. These include good nutrition, good relationships, preventive medicine such as Septrin (co-trimoxazole), and treatment of illnesses that do appear.

Timing

Let us think again about the course of HIV infection. First is the beginning, with no sign or perhaps with a mild illness. Then there are usually several years—even ten or more years—when the person is completely healthy even though carrying the infection. Finally the person begins to have symptoms such as diarrhoea, fever, and rashes, and then more serious illnesses.

When is the right time to begin taking ARVs? At the beginning? After a year or two, while the person is still healthy and fine? Later when he or she is quite sick? Doctors and researchers are still looking carefully at these questions. The short answer at present is that people should not begin taking ARVs until their immune system begins to weaken, but before they become ill with AIDS. Here are four reasons for this:

- Resistance is more likely the longer the person takes the drugs. Thus if someone begins early on, the drug may become useless before it is really needed.
- Most of the drugs have side effects—unpleasant or sometimes dangerous problems. For example, one can cause anaemia, while another can cause painful kidney stones. People who are still feeling fine will not want to take drugs that make them feel sick.
- The drugs are still costly, though the cost is decreasing. No one wants to pay to take a drug every day for ten years unless it is truly necessary. Even if the drugs are

free, there are still costs in time and money, such as transport to the clinic.

For all these reasons, the person with HIV must have a good partnership with the doctor or health worker, to observe the progress of the infection and decide when to start ARVs. Some factors are how the person is feeling, symptoms such as fever and weight loss, infections, and laboratory tests such as the CD4 count. This CD4 count is a blood test that shows how many of the special CD4 white blood cells are in the body. Where the CD4 count is not available, the doctor may observe, instead, the number of white blood cells called lymphocytes. When either the CD4 count or the lymphocyte count falls to a certain number, it is time to consider starting ARV therapy.[102]

A special test, called the "viral load," measures the amount of virus in the body and indicates how fast it is multiplying. Viral load testing is only available in high-powered laboratories.

Before making the decision to begin treatment with ARVs, the person should be sure to have a clear discussion with the health care worker covering these issues. It is not right simply to begin taking ARVs only because one has a positive HIV blood test.

Commitment

Let us say that you are the one considering taking ARVs, and that you have discussed these issues with your health care worker. What else do you need to think of? Mainly, you must remember that this is a long-term commitment. Think of it like marriage. You must not begin the treatment unless you are committed to continuing it. Remember that if you choose to

---

[102] Doctors are still debating at what CD4 count treatment should be started. The answers will doubtless change as we learn more. Current (2004) recommendations are to start ARV when the CD4 count is less than 200 (some say a little lower, some say as high as 350). The issues are complex and the answers are not all available yet.

wait, you can always begin later. But if you start and stop, start and stop, or take the drugs only most of the time, your condition could worsen. You could develop resistant virus, making the drugs useless for you. So, consider these issues:

- Cost: will you be able to continue paying for the drugs?
- Reliable source: will you be able to keep getting the drugs regularly? Do you have confidence in the clinic or pharmacist to provide original and unspoiled drug? There have been reports of fake antiretroviral drugs being sold to the people living with AIDS.
- Possible side effects: are you willing to live with the annoying problems these drugs might cause you, such as rash or stomach problems? Your health care worker will help you deal with these and lessen them, but you still must accept some problems.

In truth, you may never be confident of all these things. There are too many uncertainties. But you should do your best to answer these questions as well as you can before starting ARV treatment. For example, you may not know whether you can pay for the drug for two years, but know you can pay for six months. That is better than beginning when you can only pay for one month.

Will the drugs help?

In your decision whether to start ARV treatment, you should think of how the drugs may help you. The goal is to stop the virus from destroying the immune system. If the drugs are successful, you can expect to have fewer symptoms of HIV, fewer infections and better ability to fight off illnesses. By God's grace and with the help of the drugs, you may be able to continue working longer and caring for your children and loved ones. You may not need to be spending much time in hospital.

Everyone is different, of course, but in general someone who starts taking ARVs at the proper time will be able to lead a healthier life than one who does not take them.

Side effects

Antiretroviral drugs are strong because they are fighting a strong and clever enemy. Sometimes, they cause problems for the human body. The problems are not usually serious, but it is important to be aware of them for at least two reasons.

- People taking ARVs should know to expect problems, and not be frightened or discouraged from taking the drugs when problems come. They should not say, "Oh, this drug causes my head to ache, so it must be bad for me." No, they should know from the beginning that headaches might come. It is not a surprise. It might be part of the price of taking this valuable drug. As with any drug, people need to consider the advantages and disadvantages.
- People should also know that some problems can be serious. It is important always to tell the health care worker of any problems that happen while taking the drug. The health care worker can discuss the problems with you and determine whether they are serious. For example, a headache may be unpleasant, but is probably not dangerous. Yellowness of the eyes, however, may not be unpleasant at all but could be dangerous. Be sure to tell the health care worker about any problems you are having whether or not you think that the drugs are the cause.

Every drug has its own possible side effects and we cannot list them all here. Instead we will list some of the more common and important ones. Sometimes it is not clear whether the problem is caused by the drug, by HIV or by something else. Happily, side effects such as headache and abdominal problems that bother a person at the beginning of treatment will often disappear after some time. But remember to discuss *any* new symptom with your health care worker.

Common side effects:

- Abdominal problems: mild diarrhoea, gas, fullness, indigestion, pains, nausea, vomiting.
- Headache
- Rashes
- Tingling, burning, other pains caused by damage to nerves.

Less common side effects:

- Liver problems
- High sugar or lipids (fats) in the blood, or both
- Anaemia
- Change in body appearance. The arms and face may become skinny, while fat moves to the abdomen.

Of course, ARVs do not protect anyone from all illnesses and body troubles! The person taking ARVs can still become ill with malaria, diarrhoea, catarrh, pneumonia and so on, just as anyone can.

Things to consider during antiretroviral treatment

Starting ARV treatment is a big decision. The possibility of new health and strength is a precious gift not to be wasted. If you are taking ARVs, how can you do your part to make the treatment successful? If a loved one is taking ARVs, how can you help them? Only by all of us working together can we have the best success.

- Work out a plan for how to be sure to take all the doses of the drug and not forget any. Who will remind you? Some ideas:

  o Find someone else who is on ARVs and agree to remind each other and check on each other.

  o Use a "pillbox" where you can put the tablets for each day of the week into separate compartments. This will show you whether you are taking each dose.

  o Mark on a chart or calendar each time you take your dose.

- Carefully follow the instructions of the health care worker or doctor. It is best if the health worker gives you written instructions so that you do not forget the details. If he or she does not give you written instructions then you should write notes yourself. Be sure to know the answers to these questions:

  o What is the name of the medicine or medicines?

  o How many tablets (or capsules or how much liquid) are to be taken and at what times? Be careful! For example, if the instructions are to take one tablet in the morning and one at night, it is not right to take two at night. The timing may be important.

  o Can the medicine be taken with food, or must it be taken on an empty stomach? Some medicines must be taken with food, others only on an empty stomach, and others at any time.

  o If the medicine is in tablet form, can the tablets be crushed if necessary? If it is a capsule, can it be broken and emptied? Sometimes, people have difficulty swallowing tablets or capsules. A few medicines should not be crushed or emptied, so check with the health care worker first.

o Are there any other drugs that do not mix well with your ARV medicines? If you are taking any other drugs, be sure to tell the health care worker. Some drugs, especially rifampicin for tuberculosis, may not mix well with some ARVs.

o What symptoms or problems might the drug cause?

o What danger signs should cause you to contact the health care worker?

- *Do not stop taking an ARV drug unless you have first talked to your doctor or health care worker.* This is very important. Your health care worker can help you decide whether you should stop the drug. If you think the drug is causing some problem, tell the worker. Perhaps the problem is not important. The health care worker may be able to show you how to reduce the problem. If the problem is too serious, the worker can help you decide whether to take a different ARV or what to do next.

- *Do not miss doses.* Remember, the drugs are only keeping the virus asleep in their cell. If you miss doses, you are allowing the virus to wake and search for the keys to the prison. Every time you miss doses, you increase the risk of making the drug forever less useful for you.

- Do not give the drugs to any other person. You understand by now that ARV treatment is not a light matter. If someone with HIV wants to begin treatment, they must do so only after proper consultation.

- Follow instructions about how to store the drugs. Strong heat and sunlight can damage some. A few need refrigeration.[103]
- Do not allow your supply of drugs to finish. Be wise and go to collect more when you see the supply becoming low. If you are to collect the drugs every month, do not wait until the last day to do so, or you may find yourself without any drugs for some time.

When a family member is taking antiretroviral treatment, your encouragement is important. They may become tired or discouraged and neglect to take the drugs. You can help greatly by checking every day to see they have taken all the doses. You can encourage them by telling them how you love them. You can thank them for trying to keep healthy by taking the drugs regularly.

Caring for children on ARV treatment

ARV treatment can be valuable for children. There are special challenges in giving children any medicine, so the parents or caretakers must be patient and clever.

- Parents must supervise children of any age to see they are taking the drugs. Parents will need to give younger children the medicine directly. Older children may take it themselves, but the parent should observe them doing so.
- Children may be unable to swallow tablets and capsules. You should check with the health care worker, as mentioned above, about how the drugs can be given.
- Children may refuse the medicine because of the taste. This is not a light problem. Even adults may find it hard

---

[103] Ritonavir in particular needs refrigeration. Partly for this reason it is not used much in developing countries.

to take some drugs because the taste is so bad. It is usually not helpful to force the drug into the mouth. Forcing will make children struggle and may cause them to vomit or choke. It is better to mix the drug with some pleasant food or drink.

Trying to give medicine to struggling, crying children is stressful for parents. Be patient and remember that they are only children and do not understand well. Your anger and threats will not help. Instead, be firm but calm and caring. Older children will respond to your words of explanation and encouragement. Younger ones will be reassured by your calm and gentle voice and touch. However, you must never let the child refuse the drugs. You, not the child, are the responsible person and the one in control.

Discussion Questions

If you are discussing these questions in a group, here is a fun idea for learning. Choose two people to play the parts for each question. Take a few minutes to think, and then act out the question. The audience can help by making suggestions. When the first two "actors" are finished, two more people can try.

1. A friend tells you that she is not worried any longer about getting HIV. She has heard that the government is now providing "drugs to cure AIDS." How would you answer her?

2. Your friend with AIDS began taking ARV drugs one year ago. Now he is feeling fine and has decided to stop taking the drugs because of the cost. He also feels that God has cured him of HIV. How would you answer?

3. You are counselling a young woman who learned that her HIV test was positive. She wants to know where to get

anti-HIV drugs so she can avoid getting AIDS. How do you counsel her?

4. Your husband (or wife, or brother or sister) has been taking ARV drugs but is discouraged. They think that the drugs are causing headache and tiredness. "Some days I do not take the medicine because I feel too tired, and I need a rest. The medicine is too strong for my body." What do you say?

5. Do you think your church should help those suffering with HIV/AIDS to buy or find what they can to help ease their suffering?

The Monkeys' New Houses

Once there were three monkeys who decided to build fine new houses. They bragged to all the other animals about how fine their houses would be. Each one said,

"I am going to build the best and strongest house you have ever seen. I will live in it for the rest of my life."

The other animals waited to see. Spider warned the monkeys to be careful not to build houses near to the termites because termites will destroy houses.

The first monkey found a good place for his house, but it was near the termite mound. He said, "I don't care anything about termites. They are only little things. Even if they come to my house, they will not cause any damage for a long time." So he built his fine house. Some other animals came to visit and said, "You have built a nice house. You are a clever monkey." But when Spider came to visit, he kept quiet.

The second monkey also found a good place for his house, but it was also near the termites. He said, "I am wiser than my brother. I will build my house here

by the termites, but if they come to my house I will find medicine to drive them away." He built his house near the termites. The other animals came to visit and said, "You have built a fine house. You are a clever monkey." But when Spider came to visit, he kept quiet.

The third monkey also liked the same place near the termites. He also wanted to be near his two friends who were building their houses there. But he thought a long time about Spider's words. He said, "My brothers are not wise. I know the termites can destroy my house someday. So I will build my house far from the termites. I will also use more costly wood that is too hard for the termites to eat. My house will be smaller because the wood will cost more, but my house will last a long time." So he built a smaller house, far from the termites, and with hard wood. The other animals

came to visit and said, "You have built a fine house also. You are a clever monkey." Spider said, "Well done."

After a few months, the termites were happily living in the house of the first monkey. He did not mind them. "They are so small. And I do not see many of them, only a few now and then. I am sure they are not harming my house." Spider warned him, "The termites are eating your house. Take care!" But Monkey did not listen. After two years his house fell on him in the night, and he died.

The termites came into the house of the second monkey also. He saw a small heap of dust and asked Spider about it. "The termites are eating your house. Take care!" Spider said.

"What can I do?" asked the second monkey.

Spider told him how to find some special leaves in the

bush, how to mix and cook them, and how to paint them onto the wood of his house. He told monkey how to burn some other leaves inside the house each night. "The smoke will drive away some of the termites. You will not like the smoke and it will make you cough. But it will help keep away the termites."

Spider also warned the second monkey, "The medicine will not kill all the termites. No medicine can do that because the termites are also clever and they hide deep in the wood and in the earth. Some day your house will fall. Take care!"

The monkey listened to Spider and did as he said. He gathered medicine from the bush and painted it onto the wood of his house. He made medicine smoke every night also, even though it made him cough all night. The termites seemed to go away for a time, or to be hiding deep in the wood, but they were slowly destroying the house. After seven years the house fell down in the night, and the second monkey died.

The third monkey went with Spider and the other animals to the burial of the second monkey. The animals asked the third monkey if he was afraid of his house falling. "No, my house will not fall. My house is far from the termites, and the wood  is too hard for them. The termites have never come near my house."

The third monkey grew very old and wise. All his children and grandchildren and great-grandchildren loved to come and hear him tell about how he had built his fine house, where he still lives today.

The termites in the story are like HIV. The termites destroyed the first monkey's house after only two years. Likewise HIV/AIDS will kill most infected people after a few years (but more than two, usually).

The second monkey is like someone who is infected but who takes antiretroviral drugs. The drugs will slow the infection. The person will probably live longer and will not become sick so soon. Maybe, for example, he might live for ten or twenty years instead of five years. The drugs he or she takes will likely cause some problems just as the termite medicine did (coughing from the smoke). Still, in the end, the person will probably die from AIDS.

The third monkey is like someone who is careful not to become infected at all. They know that if they become infected, they will never be able to cure the infection. The virus, like termites, will always be in the body even when hiding. Because this person is careful to avoid becoming infected, the body remains healthy and strong.

Discussion Questions

1. Do you think the second monkey knew from the beginning that "termite medicine" would only slow the termites?

2. Do you think the first monkey would have used the "termite medicine" if he had known about it?

3. Would the first and second monkeys have been more careful if they had had more information?

4. How would you answer a friend who says, "Why worry about HIV/AIDS? If I get HIV I will take the new medicines that I can get from the pharmacist or the doctor."

Esther's Parents Do Not Understand Her

Esther, who was 16 years old, knew she was attractive to men. As a Christian, she also knew she should resist the temptation of sexual sin. In fact, she was resisting the temptation. Sadly, her parents were no help to her. They did not understand her struggles and never talked to her about the temptations she faced while growing up. They rarely talked about anything else in her life either. At times, the only words that she heard from her mother were words of scolding and scorn. Somehow, she could never please her parents no matter how hard she tried. She doubted if they loved her at all. She longed to feel loved.

One day after school, Esther's English teacher called her to stay and talk to him. After twenty minutes of talking, Esther realised he had called her not to talk about English, but because he wanted her for sex. Something inside said she should be flattered, but a stronger voice told her God would not be pleased. She made an excuse about hurrying home and left the classroom as quickly as she could.

Relieved that she had made that good decision, she was walking home when her boyfriend Jacob met her. They were good friends, but Jacob was becoming more demanding of her. He was jealous of the teacher's obvious liking for Esther, so he thought he would try to seduce her too. He told her that he loved her and thought she was beautiful. Esther thought that she loved Jacob too, but knew God did not want her to give in to him. Jacob said he wanted to show Esther how much he loved her. He wanted to prove to her that he was a man. He told her that if she really loved him, she would say yes to sex. Once again, Esther refused. She was happy in her heart that God had helped her to make a good decision.

Jacob left her, and she hurried towards home. She was pleased with herself for once again refusing the temptation before her. Yet she longed to be loved by someone. She was already about one hour later than usual in getting home from school. What would her mother say?

As she hurried along the road towards her house, but still just outside the town, a friend of the family came by in his beautiful, shiny red Mercedes. His name was Matthew. He was a businessman, and was well dressed in his dark suit, clean white shirt, and colourful tie. He looked so handsome. Exciting music boomed from the car. Matthew looked at Esther with longing, pleading eyes. He spoke softly to her, telling her she was so beautiful, and offered to drive her home. However, Esther knew by the way he was eyeing her that he had more on his mind than just a drive home. Even though she was now very late, she refused to ride with Matthew. When he drove off in a cloud of dust, she knew she had made a good decision. She said to herself, "Today I have made three good decisions."

Esther opened the front door quietly, hoping to move quickly into her room without her mother noticing that she was late coming home. However, it was not to be. Her mother was ready for her. She caught Esther's school blouse and jerked her so hard that she tore the cloth. She beat Esther with a stick. She shouted "You

useless girl. I know where you have been. I know that you have been with your men. You wicked girl. You will not stay under my roof. Get out and don't come back!" Esther tried to explain about why she was late but her mother would not listen.

Esther left the house. For a while, she stood outside the compound thinking. Then she walked slowly back to town. She felt rejected, misunderstood and unloved. She hung her head and wept. She had tried so hard today to live a good life. However, her mother did not even try to listen or understand. She would find Jacob. At least he loved her. Esther stayed with an uncle in the town. She did not go home.

By the time Esther's mother inquired of her daughter again, several weeks had passed. Esther was already pregnant. In addition, Jacob, knowing that she was pregnant, was no longer interested in her. Esther began living a rough life in order to survive away from home and take care of her baby. Esther eventually contracted HIV and, years later, died of AIDS, leaving her child an orphan on the street.

Discussion Questions

1. How might the story have been different if Esther's mother had taken time to listen and understand what was happening in her daughter's life?

2. Discuss life skills (words and actions) which could help someone like Esther to escape each of the temptations she met.

3. What life skills might have helped Esther deal effectively with life at home?

Chapter Thirteen
What About Condoms?

There is no doubt that condoms, used properly and consistently, do substantially reduce the risk of transmitting HIV/AIDS. However, they do not eliminate that risk. Most condom failure is from incorrect use or inconsistent use. Some people will insist on having sexual relationships before or outside marriage, and will refuse to take the loving correction of family members and friends. Certainly such foolish people should insist on condom use with every sexual encounter. It could save their lives.

Not everyone in Africa is going to listen to the Christian message of abstinence before marriage and faithfulness in marriage. If someone insists on having sex outside marriage and uses a condom, it will reduce some of the physical risks of the immoral behaviour.

Condoms provide some protection. Using a condom does not make the sexual sin better or worse in God's eyes, but might prevent someone from getting AIDS. Sadly, however, condom use is often emphasised at the expense of abstinence and faithfulness. Sometimes, it seems that funding agencies do not believe that Africans can abstain from sex before and outside marriage, and so the agencies put all of their funds into promoting condoms and not abstinence.

We ask our readers to understand that we are writing about condom use, because we do believe that condoms can have a place in lowering the risk of HIV infection. They can be especially useful in marriage when a partner is infected. However, they are not the complete answer the advertisers claim they are. The best estimates indicate that condoms are about 80 percent effective in preventing HIV transmission.[104] That is good, but it means that 20 percent of the risk is still present.

Condoms in marriage

Sometimes, people have such a negative view of condoms that even those who *are married* feel they cannot use them to prolong or save their lives. However, the use of condoms in marriage is important when one partner is infected with HIV or is worried that the other may be infected due to unfaithfulness outside of the marriage. They are also useful when couples want to leave spaces between their children, or to stop having children. Couples are more likely to use condoms consistently and correctly in this situation than before marriage, especially when the HIV status of the couple is known.

Even though their sexual union as a married couple is lawful in God's eyes, this union is unsafe when HIV is present and may eventually lead to the death of both partners. Consistent and correct condom use in this marriage will greatly reduce this risk. It is also important for the couple to learn other ways of expressing love and sexual feelings (see page 234).

---

[104] Weller, S. and K. Davis., Condom Effectiveness in Reducing Heterosexual HIV Transmission. *Cochrane Database Syst Rev* (1): CD003255, 2002.

A couple should use condoms even when they are both infected, for two reasons. The *first reason* is to prevent pregnancy. A baby from this union would either die with HIV or be left as an orphan when still young.

The *second reason* is that one spouse may have or develop a more dangerous strain (type) of virus than the other spouse, and it could pass to the other spouse. For example, the wife's immune system may be dealing for a time with the HIV strain that is in her body, while the virus in the husband becomes more aggressive. If the wife gets the more aggressive strain of HIV from her husband, it may overwhelm her immune system.

Condoms can make sex safer within marriage, but the risk is still present. If testing before marriage shows that an engaged person is infected with HIV, cancelling the wedding may be wiser, though this needs to be the couple's decision made after careful counselling.

Correct condom use

Someone using a condom must be sure to use it correctly, or it will be of no use. Condoms are made of latex, a rubber product also used to make surgeons' gloves. They are sensitive to heat, light and aging, so you must check to be sure they are in good condition. First, check to see that the packaging is in good order, not damaged or torn. The companies put an air bubble inside the condom packaging to help protect it from being damaged. If the bubble is not there, the condom will be damaged. Press the package. It should feel "squishy" and spring back when you press it. Check that the expiry date on the package has not passed. Open the package carefully to avoid damaging the condom. Check the condom itself. It should not be brittle (easily broken) or discoloured.

A condom should be rolled onto the erect penis of the husband *before* any contact is made between husband and wife. This prevents from the start any contact between the fluids of the penis and the vagina. A condom comes tightly rolled up and will only unroll one way. First, squeeze out the air from the "teat" at the end of the condom, leaving space for the semen to collect after it comes out. Use one hand to hold the teat and the other hand to roll the condom over the entire erect penis. Take care not to pierce the condom with nails or jewellery. Use only a water-based lubricant such as KY Jelly. Never use Vaseline or petroleum jelly as these will destroy the condom.

After intercourse, the husband should withdraw from his wife immediately and hold the condom to prevent its slipping off. Then, he must remove the condom carefully so as not to spill any of the semen. He should dispose of it in a latrine, burn it, or put it somewhere else where children will not play with it. A *new* condom *must* be used every time the couple has sexual intercourse together, even if that happens during the same night. Some people may try to use a condom more than once, but they are risking their lives.

Is safe sex possible using a condom?

Organisations and manufacturers are promoting a myth when they say that "safe sex" is possible using a condom. They are leading our young people astray. The only safe sex is between two people who are not infected. In one advertisement a Super Eagles football star says, "Play Safe. Use a condom." He could say "play safer" or "make sex safer," or "lower the risk when having sex," rather than say "Play Safe," and he would be nearer to the truth. In our view, indiscriminate condom promotion is like saying to our young people, *"We expect you to sin sexually, and now you can sin sexually safely."* Remember, condoms decrease the danger by 80 percent, but 20 percent of the danger remains. Condoms make sex safer, but not absolutely safe. We certainly would not trust our lives to them.

Condoms certainly *cannot* guarantee absolute protection from HIV. It is distorting the truth to call techniques "safe" when they lower but do not remove the risk of infection. "Safer" and "safe" are very different when we are addressing life and death issues.

"Moral but unsafe" versus "immoral but safe"
A story to illustrate the truth that condom use in marriage may be life saving since sexual relationships inside marriage are not always safe relationships

Two men live beside each other in the village. One is John and the other is Simon.

The first man, John, came home from the farm. He was hot and thirsty, so he went to the back of his house and drank his own water that his wife had carried from the river. She had not boiled it. It was dirty water. That very evening he had vomiting and diarrhoea and became quite ill. It was his *own* water he drank, but it did him harm. He had not stolen the water. He did nothing wrong or immoral by drinking the water, but he suffered because he did not take the precaution of boiling the water.

His neighbour Simon also came home from the farm. He too was feeling thirsty. He went to his house and found no water to drink. Therefore, he went to his neighbour's house. John was not around so Simon entered at the back door and stole some of John's river water. He carried the water home. In school, he had been taught to boil river water before drinking it, to make it safe. Therefore, even though he was thirsty, he boiled the water, let it cool and then drank it. The water was not his water. He stole it. What he did was wrong or immoral. However, he made the water safer by boiling it, and it did not do him any physical harm.

This story helps us understand some things about condom use. For John it was legal and moral for him to drink his own water, just as it would be for him to have sex with his wife. However, drinking his very own water harmed him. What if his wife was infected with HIV? Even though she was his own wife she could harm him, too, if he did not use condoms to make sex with her safer. *Sadly, sexual relationships in marriage are not always safe relationships.*

Simon entered John's house and stole John's water. It was not legal or moral for him to do that, just as it would be unlawful and very wrong for him to steal John's wife and have sex with her. However, Simon took the precaution of boiling the water and it did not make him sick. If he had stolen John's wife for sex with her, that would be illegal and very wrong. However, if he had taken the precaution of using a condom, he would have been less likely to get sick from HIV or any other sexually transmitted disease that Mrs John might have had.

Widespread condom promotion is not the answer to the AIDS problem

Here are some reasons why condoms alone will not solve the problem of the AIDS epidemic:

False security

Perhaps the main problem with encouraging condom use is that it gives people a false sense of security. They think they are now safe from all the negative results of sex. As a result, they may engage in even *more* sex than before. Since condoms are not perfect and not always used correctly, and since people are now feeling so "safe" to have promiscuous sex, the problem of HIV could actually be made worse.

"If we tell youth that if you use condoms, you will be safe, then we are actually fuelling the epidemic," said Vinand M. Nantulya, senior health adviser at the Global Fund to Fight AIDS, Tuberculosis, and Malaria, and formerly a key adviser to President Yoweri Museveni of Uganda.[105]

Also, think of the difference between failure as a contraceptive and failure as protection against HIV. If a condom sometimes fails to prevent pregnancy, the result is an unexpected child. If it sometimes fails to prevent HIV, the result is suffering and death for the family.

Let us illustrate with a story.

Three Buses in the Motor Park

One day, you go to the motor park to find a taxi or bus to take you to the capital. You want to travel there safely.

Bus 1

When you approach the first bus, which has ten seats, the driver welcomes you but sadly explains that on the journey they will likely have an accident and eight of the ten passengers will be killed! You are shocked. You will never join that bus.

---

[105] Donnelly, J., "UN Report Adds to a Condom Debate." *Boston Globe*, 22 June 2003.

Bus 2

You approach the next bus and the driver welcomes you. He explains that on the journey the passengers will be asked to wear seat belts, but sadly the bus will likely have an accident on the journey. Because of the protection by seat belts, only two or maybe three of the ten passengers may be killed. He encourages you to climb on board the bus, saying that maybe you will be one of the seven or eight to survive the journey! You are shocked and again decide the risk is too great. You could be one of the two or three to be killed on the journey, and you will not take that risk.

Bus 3

You approach a third bus. The driver welcomes you and explains that he will drive carefully, he will obey the speed limit and the road signs, and that you will get to Lagos safely. He has never had an accident. You breathe a sigh of relief, board that bus, and make the journey safely.

In this illustration, the first bus shows the risk of having casual sex here and there with no precautions at all. In today's climate of AIDS, you have a very high risk, maybe 80–90 percent, of dying from AIDS when you take no precautions at all and engage in casual sex.

The journey of the second bus shows the risk of having casual sex but using a condom. The seat belt in the story illustrates this safety measure. Wearing the seatbelt does make the journey safer, but you feel that the risk is still too high to take. The risk is lower than in the first bus, but you know that you could be one of the two or three people killed on the journey. In the same way, using condoms reduces the risk in what is still the dangerous "journey" of casual sex.

The third bus shows the life-style of someone who obeys God's laws and does not have casual sex at all. They are unlikely to ever become infected with the AIDS virus.

Condom promotion alone is an impractical message

From a social standpoint, even if we *did* believe condoms were one hundred percent safe, it would be impractical to say they should be used for all risky sex, that is, when one or both partners have had sex with someone else.

Most nations in Africa have less than three days' wages per person to spend on total health care each year. This government money has to cover a variety of medical care including hospital staff salaries and equipment, clinic treatment, and vaccination programmes. The entire health budget for one person would be used up on condoms in less than three months. The cost of "rubberising" all sex in Africa, as Dr Dixon calls it, would be at least 250 million pounds sterling per year. Even if we did have condoms for everyone, the distribution would often fail in the remote corners of Africa.

President Museveni of Uganda declared, "We cannot say that there is only a thin piece of rubber between us and the death of a continent."[106]

Young people lack the knowledge and discipline to use condoms consistently

Many of us, especially young people, are inconsistent in much of our lives. We only have to look at small things like cleaning our teeth or keeping our rooms tidy and we see inconsistency.

---

[106] quoted by his wife at Prescription for Hope conference, Washington, DC, 2002

How much more dangerous that inconsistency is in condom use! Often young people (and older ones, too) have good intentions. When they start out in a sexual relationship, they use condoms, but after some time the discipline in condom use decreases, and its importance seems less.

Young people themselves testify that they begin to use condoms in their relationships, but as time passes and trust builds (or the supply of condoms runs low), they stop using them. Then, of course, they risk transmitting or receiving the AIDS virus.

Young people also say that having condoms easily available encourages them to develop a lifestyle where having sexual relationships is the normal pattern in boy-girl relationships. Then, at times when no condoms are available, they take the risk of having unprotected sex and live to pay for that choice.

Young people also tell us condom use requires planning in a relationship. If a girl carries a condom, it makes her look "easy." Men often do not like condoms as they say they are difficult to use properly and decrease their pleasure. One man told me that it was like shaking a hand with a glove on—he was not going to do that! In the Africa, where men are usually the boss in any relationship, *they* usually make the decision about whether or not a condom is to be used. For a woman to even to discuss the use of a condom takes courage and a self-assurance that few young girls have. Any woman, even a wife, finds it difficult to talk to her partner about condoms or sex.

Promoting condoms alone can encourage people to disobey God's law

The Declaration of the All Africa Church and AIDS Consultation in Kampala, Uganda says:

> We believe that the prevention of AIDS is best promoted in God's ideal of fidelity and faithfulness in

monogamous marriage and sexual abstinence before marriage. We recognise that we can fall short of God's ideal and suffer consequences. When physical life can be preserved in the midst of consequences, we recognise that condoms may reduce risk, but we believe that promotion of condoms as the primary prevention of AIDS falls far short of God's ideal for the sanctity and joy of sexual fulfilment in marriage. We believe that the condom is not the central issue; rather it is the promiscuous behaviour that pollutes the holiness of sex and then uses the condom to escape from the consequences of sin.[107]

Apart from the risks and disadvantages of using a condom, promotion of condoms can seem like promotion of a promiscuous life style that encourages our young people to go against God's teaching on purity. In the Bible, God gives us guidelines for our lives, and he does that because he knows what is best for us. Even though condom use may lessen the problem in some instances, it is not the solution from God's perspective.

WHO and other leading bodies agree that sexual abstinence before marriage is the most effective means of controlling this disease.

The most effective way to prevent sexual transmission of HIV is to abstain, or for two people who are not infected to be faithful to one another. Alternatively, the correct use of a condom will reduce the risk significantly.[108]

Uganda has successfully used the ABC slogan and made it popular elsewhere. **A**bstinence before marriage, **B**e Faithful in

---

[107] Kampala Declaration. MAP International AIDS Brief, 3rd and 4th quarter 1994.
[108] World Health Organization on World AIDS Day, 1992.

Marriage, and if you do not do either, use a Condom. All three messages are important.

A September 2003 USAID report titled "Faith-Based Organizations: Contributions to HIV Prevention" shows that emphasis on A and B, and suitable advice on C, has led to the significant reduction in new HIV cases.[109]

The Pan African Christian AIDS Network passed this resolution in Nairobi in 2003:

> We acknowledge the need to respect the diversity within the faith community regarding prevention strategies and note the need to have expanded prevention efforts. We commit ourselves to,
>
> (a) Build capacity to deliver strong "Abstinence" and "Be Faithful" programmes, and to give appropriate and accurate information on Condoms within the context of our own faith, rather than just being perceived as anti condoms.
>
> (b) Create an environment for open discussion on prevention issues.
>
> (c) Call on clergy and laity to model abstinence before marriage and being faithful to their spouse after marriage.

> The simple answer to AIDS is an "epidemic of faithfulness."

The simple answer to AIDS is an "epidemic of faithfulness." In the words of David Cunningham of Scripture Union, "If everyone kept to God's standards for life and relationships for the next 12 years, AIDS

---

[109] Dr Edward Green, Harvard Center for Population and Development Studies, *Faith-Based Organizations: Contributions to HIV Prevention,* USAID, September 2003.

would disappear."[110] The disaster we are facing in Africa can be stopped. Let us work towards that.

The danger of having an "anti-condom" campaign instead of an anti-AIDS campaign

It is true that condoms do not guarantee absolute protection. It is also true that promoting condoms as the total answer to HIV is not right. However, we do see a danger that some well-meaning Christians become so "anti-condom" that they discourage *all* condom use. They condemn even condom use by people who are going to be promiscuous anyway, or by those who need to protect their spouse or themselves. Sadly, Christians are becoming so divided about condoms that there is a danger of losing focus. The *condoms* become the "evil thing," rather than the sexual acts that are taking place outside the bonds of marriage. *We should not waste energy or time arguing over condoms.*

Some people who campaign against condoms argue that the small virus can pass through the pores (invisible holes) of the condom. Their argument is untrue. *Many studies have shown quite clearly that HIV cannot pass through an undamaged latex condom.*[111] We need to understand clearly that condoms *do* provide much protection even though they are not perfect.

Despite their advantages in some situations, condoms are not the only answer to the AIDS public health problem, either from a medical, social or Christian standpoint. Too often, groups seem to promote condoms widely in Africa, while they see sexual abstinence as too high a standard to aim for. Therefore,

---

[110] *Towards an AIDS Free Generation,* Fellowship of Christian Students, Nigeria.

[111] "Laboratory studies have demonstrated that latex condoms provide an essentially impermeable barrier to particles the size of STD pathogens." CDC. Male Latex Condoms and Sexually Transmitted Diseases: Fact Sheet for Public Health Personnel, 2003. http://www.cdc.gov/hiv/pubs/facts/condoms.htm

they do not sponsor abstinence teaching as a real possibility in fighting the epidemic. *Abstinence from sex before marriage and faithfulness in marriage are God's way of avoiding AIDS.*

Discussion Questions

1. Discuss whether condom use can become an effective part of HIV/AIDS prevention among married couples in your culture and community.

2. What do you think can be done to protect women from HIV when they know that their husbands are not faithful?

Loraine's Personal Advice on Sugar Daddies

"There is something else which causes AIDS. That thing is Sugar Daddies. They may come to you with their mobile phones, cars, and nice clothes. Maybe at home you have a problem so when these old Sugar Daddies come to you and ask you to be their wives, you just say yes, especially young girls. THINK BEFORE YOU ACT! I tell you, when you are pregnant or you have AIDS, they are going to leave."

Loraine, Bulawayo, Zimbabwe [112]

[112] UNAIDS Case Study. *Investing in Our Future. Psychosocial Support for Children Affected by HIV/AIDS*, July 2001.

"There is something else which causes AIDS. That thing is Sugar Daddies. They may come to you with their mobile phones, cars, and nice clothes. Maybe at home you have a problem so when these old Sugar Daddies come to you and ask you to be their wives, you just say 'yes', especially young girls. THINK BEFORE YOU ACT! I tell you, when you are pregnant or you have AIDS, they are going to leave."

Loraine, Bulawayo, Zimbabwe.

* UNAIDS Best Practice Collection. Comfort and Hope: Six Case Studies on Mobilizing Family and Community Care for Children Affected by HIV/AIDS. Geneva, 1999.

Chapter Fourteen
Biblical and Pastoral Counselling of Those with HIV/AIDS

The aim of pastoral counselling is to lead people into greater maturity in Christ. The godly pastor prayerfully assesses the needs of each person he counsels, knowing that each one is unique. The pastor will try to encourage those who are weary, strengthen the weak and fearful, and comfort the grieving. Some people will have moved away from Christian truth and moral standards. Pastoral counselling aims to restore them to the kind of life God wants for them. The topic of pastoral counselling and HIV/AIDS is huge and needs a book of its own, but we will offer some short guidelines here.

> The pastor must always remember that he is a shepherd and not a judge.

The desire in counselling must always be to draw people closer to Christ, into greater knowledge of God. A pastor who wants to shame or condemn someone, driving them away from God rather than towards him, is acting from his own sinful desire and not in a godly way. There is certainly a need for confronting sin and for discipline, but the goal is repentance and restoration of fellowship, not shame, humiliation, or exclusion (2 Corinthians 2:3–11, 7:9; 2 Timothy 2:25; Hebrews 5:2; 1 John 5:16).

Good counselling in the area of HIV helps give people courage to bear personal responsibility for their actions and decisions, especially if sinful behaviour caused them to be infected. The pastor or counsellor should act with concern and love, confronting those they are counselling in order to help them change their behaviour and increase their understanding (Matthew 18:15; Romans 15:4; Galatians 6:1–2; Psalm 19:7–14; 2 Timothy 3:16–17; Hebrews 4:12; 2 Peter 1:3–4).

Many people who were infected through immoral behaviour have great difficulty admitting that fact. They often say they were infected by the barber or through some other unlikely circumstance. If someone did have sexual intercourse before or outside of marriage, the counsellor should encourage them to admit to that and to ask God for forgiveness. They may also need to ask forgiveness from their spouse. If they continue to deny the behaviour, they cannot truly know God's forgiveness and peace.

> Good counsellors must keep confidentiality.

Pastoral counselling should also encourage and equip people to help others in the same way as they are being helped. The pastor cannot meet all the counselling needs in his congregation, because there are too many people with too many needs. If he trains helpers, though, they can also have the opportunity to meet the needs of the congregation. They will learn that God's word is powerful and sufficient in addressing any problem. As in all counselling situations, the counsellors must be one hundred percent trustworthy in keeping confidentiality (2 Peter 1:2–11; Galatians 6:5; 2 Timothy 3:16, 17; 2 Corinthians 1:3–5).

The problems of HIV/AIDS touch all of us, whether we are pastors, counsellors, doctors, people living with HIV, or family members. When we face the problems, it is easy for us to react in a human way rather than in God's way. We need to see the problems as God does. Often, the natural way to handle the problem is to give in to our selfish instincts and to try to shift responsibility for the problem to circumstances or to others. We act as if we are pure, innocent, and good at heart. We believe and claim that outside forces or influences are to blame for our condition. We often blame the devil. People say, "The devil made me do it." God's way, though, is to take responsibility for our actions and, if necessary, come to repentance and forgiveness. Only then can we truly move on towards healing and acceptance in that situation.

Those infected or affected by HIV/AIDS need biblical hope. God promises that he will not let anyone face problems he or she cannot handle. He promises to provide help and direction in every situation as we aim to deal with the problem in his way (1 Corinthians 10:13; Romans 8:28; Hebrews 13:5).

Infected or affected people need also to know what God wants them to do and how God wants them to react. Even if their lives are being shortened, life is not yet finished. Whether counsellor or counselee, not one of us knows the day when God will allow our lives to end. No matter how many days we have left on earth, we must each live each and every day to the glory of God.

The godly counsellor helps people with HIV/AIDS see that God still has plans, blessings, and a calling for them. For example, the pastor or counsellor can help them to use God's word in the situations they face every day. This can include dealing with negative or destructive thoughts, fear, and depression. It can include learning to forgive those who have caused the pain and asking forgiveness of those we have hurt. We all need to have biblical patterns of thought, word and action to help us live in a way that pleases God (Ephesians 4:22–23; James 1:22–25; 1 Peter 3:8–12).

People who are learning to live positively with HIV/AIDS can make a valuable contribution by counselling others facing some of the same struggles as they are facing. The church can use people with HIV/AIDS who are finding God's strength and comfort to visit and counsel those struggling with fears and questions. This helps strengthen the faith of both groups. Many people living with HIV/AIDS use a "buddy system" to keep each other accountable in taking their medications and in living in a way that does not infect others.

HIV testing of those planning to marry

There are good reasons for couples to be tested for HIV before marriage. Several denominations in Africa have ruled that their pastors must require church members to have HIV testing before marrying in church. We hope the purpose is not to punish people, but to prevent the spread of AIDS, restore people to the path of following Christ, and care for those who are infected.

On the other hand, some Christians feel strongly that churches should not *require* HIV testing before marriage. They feel that such a requirement is discriminatory and interferes with the couple's privacy and freedom. These concerns are valid. Church leaders need to balance them with the church's responsibility for the welfare of the couple, their parents and families, and their future children.

As a pastor or elder, you should include these points when you counsel a couple planning to marry:

- what HIV is and how people contract it
- how HIV testing can help the couple
- risk factors the man and woman may have in their pasts
- the importance of sexual purity in the future, and how it will help protect the couple and their children
- assurance that you will minister God's love, grace and forgiveness to the couple regardless of the test results.

Sadly, pastors, elders and church members have often reacted with judgement and condemnation when they learn that the intending man or woman has HIV. These reactions come from fear, ignorance, and self-righteousness. We need to remember, AIDS is not spread by sexual activity only, though nine out of ten are infected by sexual activity. Having AIDS is not a sin. The person with HIV may or may not have been infected because of sin. We must also remember that even if one or both

> Having AIDS is not a sin.

parties have sinned sexually, they need to be treated with genuine concern and Christian love.

When people learn they have HIV, they enter a serious spiritual crisis—the "valley of the shadow of death." They desperately need a shepherd. Unless the pastor can counsel the intending couple in a compassionate and biblical way, he may do harm where good was intended.

The timing of the HIV test before marriage is important. The test needs to be done early in the marriage preparations and at least six months before the marriage. It is best done before the wedding is announced and before any other preparation for the wedding has begun. It is difficult for the couple to pull back from the marriage if they have printed their invitation cards, received wedding gifts, bought the food, and all the rest. It is much easier for the marriage to be cancelled if everything has not become public.

Many pastors are finding this a difficult problem. Often, by the time the couple comes to them, the bride price has already been paid and all is agreed between the families. The couple may even come to the pastor only a few weeks before the planned wedding. Perhaps the church leaders need to inform their members that every wedding must have a six-month minimum preparation time. Gradually the congregations will come to accept this.

Preparing the engaged couple for HIV testing (Pre-test counselling)

The pastor *must* prepare the couple before sending them to an HIV testing centre. This helps reduce the shock if the test is found to be positive. It also opens the door for further discussion and counselling.

To introduce the subject, the pastor can ask the couple what they know about HIV/AIDS. Then he can tell them the ways HIV spreads and ask whether they think they might be at risk from any of these ways. The couple will be more likely to respond honestly if the pastor has made clear that he wants to *help* them have a healthy relationship, and is not acting as a policeman.

At this point, the pastor may discover that the couple are already sexually active. He may need to counsel them about God's plan for their relationship, emphasising that when we repent, God forgives us from all sin including sexual sin. Even though he may find it difficult to talk to the couple about these issues, biblical counselling at this point can help lay a foundation for a healthier marriage and reduce problems in the future.

The pastor can also help the couple think about what their reactions would be if one or the other were found to be HIV positive. This is important preparation for the time when the test results are disclosed.

All through this counselling, the pastor must help the couple to understand the true purpose of doing the HIV test. That purpose is to protect their intended loved one from becoming infected and to help them to make an informed choice about their future. It must not be to punish, condemn or discard the infected person. The pastor should assure the couple that he will continue ministering God's love, grace and forgiveness to them regardless of the test results.

Counselling engaged couples when the HIV test for both the man and woman is negative

With the commonness of HIV in our times, the couple will rejoice when both their test results are negative. The wise pastor will use this time to encourage the couple. If they have been abstinent, he should praise them for their good sexual behaviour and encourage them to continue to abstain from sexual activity until after the marriage. If they have already been having sex or were sexually active in the past, he can use this time to help them come to repentance and assurance of forgiveness.

Whether or not the couple have been abstinent, the pastor can use Scripture to show them God's plan for the sexual relations of the husband and wife. That plan is that they always remain faithful to each other in the years ahead (1 Corinthians 7:1–3, 5). The pastor should also show them what God says about the dangers of sex outside marriage (Proverbs 5:3–5, 18; Proverbs 6:28; Proverbs 6:32; Proverbs 5:23; Proverbs 6:25; Ephesians 5:3–5; 1 Thessalonians 4:3, 7, 8; 1 Corinthians 6:9; Hebrews 13:4; Hebrews 12:16).

Counselling engaged couples when the HIV test is positive in one of them

It is easy for the pastor to be judgmental when the man or woman is found to have HIV. He must remember, though, that sex is not the only way HIV can be passed on. He must always remember that having AIDS is not a sin. HIV-infected people he counsels may never have been sexually active at all. They may have been sexually abused or raped. They may have been sexually active before coming to know the Lord Jesus as Saviour. They may have long since repented of and been forgiven for sexual sin. *HIV positive people are not necessarily greater sinners than any other church member*, and the pastor must not treat them with condemnation or disrespect.

The pastor must be compassionate as Jesus is. Jesus confronted sin clearly, but lovingly called sinners to repentance and to restored, joyful fellowship. Often this is the time for the pastor to lead the person to confession, forgiveness and restoration, if that is what is needed. It is also the time to bring words of comfort and reassurance.

> AIDS is a disease and not a sin.

Many pastors feel that the compassionate thing to do is to *not* perform the wedding, knowing that the risk to the uninfected partner in the relationship is great. Perhaps you can imagine a situation where you know there are armed robbers on the road and your friend is in danger of losing his life there. You do not warn him. You act as if there is no danger. You say to yourself, "I do not want to make my friend fearful, so I will not tell him." Would that be compassionate? The right thing is to tell your friend about the dangers ahead. That would be the loving and compassionate thing to do.

The pastor needs to be sure that the couple understand the issues:

- If they proceed with the marriage, the infected partner is almost sure to eventually infect the other one, and both will die from AIDS.
- Condom use in marriage will probably greatly lengthen the lifetime of the uninfected partner.
- If they try to have children (frequent intercourse without a condom), the uninfected partner will likely become infected quickly.
- Children born to them have a 30 percent chance of being infected from mother-to-child transmission, unless there is access to antiretroviral drugs and a safe substitute for breast-feeding.
- Even if the babies are not infected, they will eventually be left as orphans.

However, some couples feel that they love each other so much they cannot face life without each other. They want to proceed with the marriage, no matter what the result is. The pastor should encourage the couple to make their decision slowly rather than rush ahead. He should pray with them and for them. He should encourage them to be honest with each other. For their best, they need to make their decisions with God's guidance. God wants the best for his children.

The uninfected partner has a hard decision to make. Sometimes that partner feels willing to risk life for love. He or she may desire to care for the infected partner, even if it means a shorter life.

Sometimes the infected partner decides in genuine love and care not to have sexual relations with the loved one. He or she may choose to show love by not getting married, but remaining friends.

The pastor cannot stop the couple from being married, but it is his own decision before God whether or not he wants to perform the wedding ceremony. The couple must make an informed decision, and the pastor must keep the information he now knows completely to himself. It is tempting for the pastor to tell others, but no one else needs to know. There is no reason why even the elders of the church need to know the couple's HIV status. No one is at risk from social contact with the infected person. If the engaged couple want to share the news with others, they themselves can do so.

Recently, I heard of one young man who did not know that he was HIV positive since he and his fiancée had not yet gone back to his pastor for their post-test interview. On the

> The pastor or counsellor must keep all information confidential.

street, he met someone who said he was sorry for his bad news! The pastor had not kept the information confidential. As a result, he lost the trust of his congregation. There is no excuse for such gossip.

The pastor would be wise to involve the parents of the intending couple in the decision of whether or not to proceed with the wedding. He should ask the permission of the couple to approach the parents. If he does not involve the parents, the parents of the uninfected one may become angry when they discover that the pastor knew of the HIV infection and still continued with the wedding without involving them. I have heard of a pastor being assaulted by angry parents for knowingly marrying their HIV negative daughter to an HIV positive man!

Parents may help their children approach the questions with more perspective and wisdom. Sometimes, the young couple themselves think their strong love will overcome all the problems HIV could bring. Or they may believe God will heal the infected one. The parents may have a more realistic view of things to come. They do not have the same range of emotions that the young couple have. There are many good reasons for involving the parents, but the pastor must first have the couple's consent.

If there are medical issues that the pastor does not feel competent to discuss with the couple, he should feel free, with the couple's permission, to refer them to a medical person for further help.

If they decide to marry, they may want advice about how to show sexual love to each other in a risk-reducing way. They need to know the information given in Chapter Thirteen about condoms. By touching and kissing, they can give each other sexual pleasure and even climax (orgasm) without full sexual intercourse (see Sex without 'Sex' on page 234). They need advice about covering cuts on the hands with waterproof dressings to avoid the virus in the sexual fluids entering through cuts or breaks in the skin. The risk of getting HIV from a sexual partner is greatest in the first few months after that person becomes infected. There is also great risk towards the end of the infected person's life, because of the increasing level of virus in his or her blood and sexual fluids.

When the time comes for practical help and care of the infected person, the body of Christ, the church, must be willing to do what Jesus would do. In Jesus' name, the church must offer the suffering individual and family hope of eternal life in Christ, forgiveness of sins through his sacrifice for sin, and practical love through care and service. As Christians we have real hope in Jesus Christ even in the midst of something as devastating as HIV/AIDS. He is our "Prescription for Hope."

It is tempting to offer false hope to the infected person and to assure them God will heal them. God certainly can heal. He is an all-powerful God, and sometimes he does heal people with AIDS. We need to pray for this healing. However, healing does not often happen, and we must not talk as if we know God's will for everyone in the matter of healing.

The pastor should help the couple understand that with a healthy life style, the infected partner could live for years, especially if the HIV infection is in the early stage. (See *What are the stages leading to AIDS?* starting on page 16 for a review of the course of HIV infection.) If antiretroviral drugs are available and used properly, an even longer lifetime is possible.

Reactions of those found to have HIV infection

In my experience, many people who learn that they are infected with HIV do not believe the result of the blood test. They are shocked and will want to repeat the test. Even when the second test confirms the first, they may go through a period of denying the truth of their situation. Indeed, they may "know" that it is not possible. Often they are angry with God and with whoever was responsible for their infection. After a repeated test, they will often run here and there looking for cures for HIV/AIDS. They may spend large sums of money on herbs, so-called vaccines, or other unproven methods in the hope of a cure. They may even try bargaining with God, promising that they will pray and give and work for him if only he will cure them.

The pastor may need to gently and firmly guide people through this period of shock, denial and anger and on to acceptance of their condition. People make progress in their own time, and the counsellor should be sensitive to that timing. Do not try to rush them into acceptance on *your* timetable, even if you feel uncomfortable with their anger or confusion. By being with them, listening to them, and accepting them, you will help them towards a mature reliance on God's grace. The human brain and heart simply need time to absorb and process these serious events.

The Bible tells us in 2 Corinthians 4:16–18 that even when we suffer physically, there is no need to lose heart. God is renewing us inwardly day by day. The support of Christian friends is essential when the person feels lonely, rejected and perhaps depressed. As time passes and HIV positive people find that they are not going to die of AIDS in the near future, they can use the rest of their lives for God and have real hope in him. We should never underestimate the value of prayer and Christian fellowship and the strength of the Holy Spirit to empower us in these difficult situations.

As a personal testimony, I have seen occasions when singing and reading God's Word with someone who is suffering because of AIDS has brought the person great comfort and assurance that nothing can separate him or her from the love of Christ.

Counselling engaged couples when the HIV test is positive for both

Much of the previous section is equally useful when the man and woman are both HIV-infected. Because *both* are infected, they may decide that they want to proceed with the wedding. That they are both infected may or may *not* be because they have been having sex together, and the pastor must not jump to conclusions. It is the pastor's decision whether he feels right before God about performing their wedding, but no matter what he decides, he must keep the knowledge of their HIV status to himself.

Do not rush to cancel the wedding....

It is premature and unbiblical to rush into cancelling the wedding of two infected people and to exercise church discipline without knowing whether the couple are walking with God, are truly Christians, and have the fruits of the Spirit in their lives. I repeat, it is possible that this couple did not become infected through sex. Or if they did, it may have happened many years before they repented and came to know the Lord Jesus as Saviour. It is tragic when what was meant to be known only by the pastor and the couple becomes public knowledge. This causes the couple and congregation to lose confidence in the pastor's trustworthiness.

Once again, the pastor must act with great love, gentleness and genuine compassion. He must offer hope in Christ for forgiveness of sin, strength for each day, and a future in heaven. If the pastor wants to do God's work in this situation, he will not drive the couple away, but will instead try as much as is in his power to include them in the body of Christ. He has a big job ahead of him to continue to minister to these members of the body who need his support more than ever.

As discussed in the previous section, the pastor must discuss what it will mean for the babies should the woman become pregnant, dealing with their chance of infection and their certainty of becoming orphans.

Another important point is that if the couple decide to marry, they should be advised to use condoms during every act of sexual intercourse, both to prevent pregnancy and to reduce the rate at which the couple will continue to re-expose each other to HIV. The virus changes at different rates in each person's body, and the more often they re-expose each other to HIV during sexual intercourse, the more they might shorten each other's lives. In the long term of a marriage relationship, it seems unrealistic to tell them to abstain from sexual relations, but they can also be guided in other ways to show love to one another, apart from having sexual intercourse (see page 234).

The pastor or counsellor should encourage the HIV positive couple to eat a healthy diet, get enough rest, seek medical help promptly for any infections they encounter, and continue normal life for as long as possible. They should practise good hygiene, keeping themselves and their clothes, bedclothes, and room clean.[113]

Psychological and spiritual help for people living with HIV/AIDS

People living with HIV/AIDS live "in the valley of the shadow of death." Living perhaps closer to death than most of us, they often have serious questions, concerns, and fears about life, death, God, salvation, and other issues of ultimate importance. The pastor can help people with these concerns. He should be ready to listen with respect and a non-judgmental attitude. In this way, the pastor can best minister the love of Christ and offer hope and forgiveness. He can lead people to a true knowledge of God's grace and to seeing death as a gateway to heaven. Reading God's word with those who are suffering, praying together, and answering their questions are important. We often underestimate the power of prayer to bring change into the lives of suffering people. God is a God of comfort and healing. If it is his will, God can use the prayers of his people to bring healing to the person with AIDS.

---

[113] The ECWA AIDS Ministry leaflet, "Home Based Care for the Person with HIV/AIDS."

Repentance and forgiveness

Before the person with HIV/AIDS can know God's forgiveness and acceptance into God's family, he or she needs to *repent*. Repentance and faith are the only way any of us can to go to heaven. All of us need to repent in the same way as the person with AIDS. Because people are dying from AIDS does not put them into a different category. All of us are sinners (1 John 1:8, 9), whether we think our sins are "big" or "small."

God is just and holy and punishes sin. We cannot escape by claiming that we have done only "little sins." That is like saying we have only "a little HIV" in our body. The result of a little or much HIV is the same, and so it is with sin.

God is merciful and has provided us a way of escape from his anger against sin. That is through faith in Jesus Christ. He took the punishment for our sins, dying on the cross so that we could have eternal life rather than punishment.

The Bible tells us God loves us even though we are sinners (Romans 5:8). It tells us faith in Jesus Christ is the only way we can have a right relationship with God (John 14:6). It assures us that all who repent and call on God to save them will be saved and become children of God (Romans 10:13, John 1:12).

What does it mean to repent? Repentance means

- recognising the authority of God and the rightness of his words and commands
- having a true understanding that we have acted wrongly and broken God's law
- realising we are thus guilty before God
- feeling regret and sorrow for our wrongdoing
- turning *away* from sin with grief and hatred of it
- turning *towards* God, wanting with all our heart to be obedient to him

When we repent, trust in God to save us by the death and resurrection[114] of Jesus, and make him the master and authority in our lives, God saves us and brings us into his family. He forgives our sins and gives us eternal life.

Counselling the married couple living with HIV

Few things can be more painful and damaging for a couple than learning that one or both of them is infected with HIV. At best, if only one is infected, the couple face the death of the one spouse and the difficulty of coping before and after that loss. At worst, both spouses and the children may be infected, so they are looking at the end of the entire family. Few things could be a greater shock. It is important for the godly counsellor, friend, or pastor to help the couple to respond to this crisis in a positive way.

Reactions to each other

After the initial shock, it will be quite natural for the spouses to be caught up in powerful emotions. This should be easy for us to understand when we consider how terrible the situation may be for them. It *may* be that the behaviour of one or both spouses has resulted in HIV and all that comes with it. The combination of guilt, anger, denial, and fear can be overwhelming.

The pain is sure to affect the counsellor as well. The temptation is to deny or quickly cover up the couple's pain, for example by assuring them that everything is going to be all right. However, this is not helpful for the couple. They have a long road ahead of them and need to start by learning to face their emotions honestly. This does not mean they should *give in* to all their feelings. For example, they need to face their anger honestly

---

[114] coming alive after his death

and place it before God, but they should not *give in* and act in a harmful or vengeful way. They should face their fears and place them before God, but they should not give themselves up to acting in a spirit of fear.

The counsellor can be helpful by explaining some of these things to the couple. He (or she) should tell them that such reactions are normal and expected and that God understands. He should help them to realise that it may take much time before their hearts will find peace, but that God will be with them through it all. The counsellor might start by reading some of the Psalms with the couple. Many of these are written from the same kind of dark situation and with the same kinds of feelings as the couple will be feeling.

Sex without 'Sex'

What is the best thing to do when one or both marriage partners is found to be HIV positive? This is a difficult problem for the couple. Sometimes people give the couple advice that they should never again have sex together. But that advice denies the reality of their problem, and couples are rarely going to follow it. More realistically, they would be wise to reduce the frequency of having sexual relations, use condoms and not have sexual relations when the woman is menstruating. If she is HIV positive, the blood will probably contain the virus. They should also avoid deep kissing as cuts on the lips or bleeding gums can be open doors for the entrance of the virus, though this risk is very low.

Often we think of "sex" as meaning only sexual intercourse, with the husband's penis actually entering the wife, leading to climax. Indeed, this is one goal of the sexual relationship as God designed it. But the relationship can and should include much more. Couples can use many, many ways to show each other love and affection and to give each other physical and sexual pleasure. These ways include:

- words and gestures
- talking and spending time together
- non-sexual touch (such as holding hands, rubbing each others' backs)
- sexual touch of all kinds (close hugging, kissing, touching each other in ways to produce sexual excitement and pleasure).

Even apart from any question of HIV, all couples can have a more satisfying and rich relationship by learning many ways of giving each other pleasure and affection. Exactly how they do that will be different for each couple. It is one of the areas in which they need to explore how to please each other. When one or both spouses have HIV, it is even more important for them to learn to please each other sexually without intercourse. They can give each other full climax (orgasm) by lovingly touching each other's sexual organs, rubbing against each other, but without the husband entering the wife. Whatever way the couple choose to bring each other to climax (orgasm), but without full sexual intercourse, they must be careful not to let the sexual fluid that comes from the penis come near the wife's vaginal area. They may still decide to have intercourse at times, even though knowing the risk. But they will decrease the risk, while still remaining lovers, if they learn to satisfy each other frequently without having complete sexual intercourse.

Condoms for married couples

When a couple living with HIV does decide to have sexual intercourse, a properly-used condom will give them some protection, as discussed on page 202 in Chapter Thirteen.

Other issues for married couples

Some of the other issues married couples with HIV face are listed below. There is not room here to discuss them in detail, but the pastor or counsellor should be careful to help the couple work through these issues and any others that arise and to plan how they will do their best to act in godly, wise ways for the best results.

- Who will take care of the children when one of us dies? What if we both die?
- Is there any way to provide for the children's future needs before that time?
- If one or more of the children is infected, will we explain that to them? When and how?
- How and when will we explain to our children that we have HIV? It will be much better for them to hear it from us than from other people. (See *Hard to Believe* on page 272)
- How can we ensure that the surviving widow will be able to keep the family property and children? Consulting a lawyer to draw up a will may be a good idea.
- How can we restore or maintain a relationship that glorifies God even in suffering?

Family decisions

The pastor may be the best person to help people with AIDS decide what should happen to their possessions when they die. For example, if they own land, who will it belong to when they die? Do they have other possessions or money that need to be willed in writing to a family member?

Decisions may also need to be made about where it is best for the person to die. Should it be in the city away from the village family and nearer medical care, or in the village with more family care and perhaps less access to medical care?

People may have strong feelings about where they want to be buried, and the family should learn these desires so that they can respect them.

Children affected by AIDS

Some parts of Africa, especially in the south, already have a severe crisis dealing with children affected by AIDS. Others are seeing only the early stage of the problem. Everywhere, the church will need to face up to the needs of orphans in the community. The pastor or counsellor should help people with AIDS make plans for what will happen to their children, if there are any. This advance planning can make all the difference for the children's future. (See Chapter Sixteen about children affected by AIDS.)

Family reconciliations

HIV/AIDS always causes stress in families, and sometimes there may be a breakdown of relationships. Maybe a husband and wife blame each other for what has happened. Or maybe they have not spoken about what the real cause of the illness is and have built walls between them. Or maybe the children are angry with their parents because they are going to die and leave the children without money or resources for food or schooling. The pastor, as an outsider to the family, can help with family communication on these issues. Good relationships and reconciliation before someone with AIDS dies help the person die more peacefully. They also help those left behind to go through the grieving process in a more healthy way and to get on with life more effectively.

Family support

During the illness and after the death of the person with AIDS, the pastor must visit the family. We hear too many stories of families grieving alone with no one caring for them just because of the stigma attached to AIDS. Instead, this is one time when we must follow Christ's command to love our neighbour (Luke 10:27). The pastor must lead the way in showing that God loves, forgives, and gives hope for the future. If the pastor is a good example, others will follow. If the pastor loves and cares, others will follow his example. But it is God's purpose that *all* Christians should care for those in need, especially for those despised by the world (Matthew 25:31–46).

Listening to the dying person and the grieving family is time-consuming, but the pastor and others in church leadership must spend time listening and comforting (2 Corinthians 1:3, 4).

The Pan African Christian AIDS Network (PACANet) passed this resolution concerning what the church should do about people living with HIV/AIDS:

> The participants resolved to understand and respect persons living with HIV/AIDS (PLWHA) and ensure their human dignity. They committed themselves to support and involve PLWHA in the fight against HIV/AIDS as crucial partners through the following:
>
> • Face the fact that stigma and discrimination are sin.
> • Follow the biblical mandate to show love, grace, compassion, care, hope, practical support, forgiveness and advocacy.

- Empower the Church with accurate and up to date facts to reduce myths and break stigma.
- Theologically and in the Church examine and practice issues related to HIV/AIDS such as compassion, forgiveness, stigma and discrimination.
- Empower and draw PLWHA as resource people for changing attitudes and developing appropriate congregational responses for the Church.
- Acknowledge the fact that there is no "them" and "us." There is only "us." Therefore the Body of Christ has AIDS.[115]

Discussion Questions

1. What policy should your church leadership have about compulsory counselling and testing before marriage? Why should they have these policies?

2. How can the HIV/AIDS epidemic be an opportunity to help to change attitudes from non-biblical to biblical?

3. Why do so many people believe that AIDS is a curse? What do you think is wrong with the attitude that believes that AIDS is a curse on bad people?

4. What is your church doing to help those with HIV/AIDS? What could your church do to help those living with HIV/AIDS, which it is not doing now?

5. Discuss ways your church could help the families of those who die from AIDS, apart from giving them money.

6. If you visited a person with AIDS, what spiritual encouragement could you give?

---

[115] Symposium on HIV/AIDS, Nairobi, 2003.

7. Discuss the special needs of children who are mourning the death of a father or mother, or even father and mother. How could the church family help?

8. You organise a club for HIV positive people. It will meet in the church. What will you do at the club? What opposition might you expect from within the congregation and how would you deal with that opposition?

Grace's Family Mourns Alone

Grace was from a small village. She became sick with AIDS when she was working in the city and went back home to her village to die. At first, the family did not know what was wrong with her, but as time passed and she became gradually more thin and weak, it became obvious that she had AIDS. The family were frightened. The village people became fearful, too, and started to talk among themselves. They stopped going to greet the family at home and talked in quiet tones amongst themselves when the subject was raised. Some no longer even greeted the family in the market. They certainly did not shake hands with them.

Even when the pastor of the church came to visit, he did not go near to Grace. He only looked around the door of her room and briefly greeted her. He refused to drink the water he was offered by Grace's mother. Inside his head, he was imagining the life Grace must have lived to allow her to become like this. He judged her without knowing any facts. He saw himself as better than she was. He thought Grace was getting what she deserved for her sin. When the people watched the pastor and how he behaved, they felt more justified in avoiding the family.

When it came to the day of the funeral, few people came and even fewer came back to the house after the burial to eat the food that had been prepared. There was no music, nor smiles, nor any feeling of hope. Grace had died condemned and alone. One hour after the burial, the compound was silent. Everyone had already gone home, leaving Grace's close family to agonise in their loss, not only of their daughter but also of a valued place in their village community. It would be a long time before they could go to the market without feeling the glare of judging eyes and hearing the whispers of maligning tongues. [116]

Discussion Questions

1. When Grace and her family were shunned, do you think that the behaviour of the community was justified? If yes, why? If not, why not?

2. If you had been Grace's pastor, what would you have done that might have helped the community to behave differently?

---

[116] Based on a true story from Nigeria

Chapter Fifteen
Home Care for a Person with AIDS

The purpose of this chapter is to help you know how to care for someone with HIV who is becoming ill or may be nearing the end of life. For years after infection, the person was an HIV carrier, though perhaps unaware of it. Finally, the immune system's defences are destroyed and the person becomes sick. He or she may have some of the early illnesses, or may be quite sick with AIDS.

AIDS affects the whole person. Fear, anger, shame and guilt often control the emotions. Friends and loved ones often cast off people with AIDS. Their partners may divorce them, their families may discard or at best ignore them, and the expense of treatment and care may place impossible burdens on everyone involved. Without good pastoral care, desperation and despair may overcome the person.

Home care is not only a way of giving comfort to the sick or dying. It is also a vitally important part of keeping the person with HIV healthy and active as long as possible. Consider the stories of Ismail and Peter.

Ismail was a welder. When he began to cough and lose weight, he went to the clinic and was told he had HIV and TB. He went home very sad. He took the anti-TB drugs for one month but then stopped because he was discouraged and because of the cost. He continued to become weaker until he could no longer work. People heard he had AIDS and would not come to visit him. With no money, the children could not continue school. They did not even have enough to eat. Ismail developed sores over his body. His wife wanted to help but did not know how, and she, too, was beginning to have cough and fever. With no encouragement, no proper food, and no health care, Ismail died six months later.

Peter was a taxi driver in the same town as Ismail. He too discovered he had HIV and TB. His HIV counsellor helped him talk to his wife, and they decided to join a support group for people living with HIV/AIDS. "Please pray for us," he asked the group. They did pray and discuss how they could help Peter and his family.

Martin volunteered to visit Peter for a short time every day. Peter and Martin would pray together and Martin would remind Peter to take the anti-TB drugs. Once, when there was not enough money for the drugs, everyone in the support group contributed a little, and it was enough to buy the drugs. Martin's wife visited Peter's wife Debora also. She told Debora what she had learned about good nutrition to help keep Martin healthy. "Take heart! You can do so much for Peter. Praise God that he is getting better from the TB and is back to work full-time."

With such caring, praying friends, Peter and Debora knew that God was with them. Peter is healthy now though he still has HIV. In fact, Peter and Debora are now visiting another family struggling with HIV/AIDS. They are passing on the encouragement and comfort that they received. Peter and Debora are planning for the future, and are praying and hoping that Peter will be able to receive antiretroviral drugs when he needs them.

People living with AIDS need to feel accepted and loved. Our becoming mature in Christ requires that we practise love and acceptance towards our suffering brothers and sisters.[117] In other words, *we* are not growing in Christ until we are loving people with AIDS as we should. Complete care takes much time, but there are some simple things anyone can do to make the sick person feel cared for. You can help by taking time to visit, talk or just sit and hold a hand. Touch is important in caring for people living with AIDS, so that they do not feel rejected. We need to care for those living with HIV/AIDS with love and dignity.

People infected with AIDS may seem content with the physical care and counsel we give them, but often in their hearts, they are crying out for words of hope and comfort. We do not serve them well if we give a high quality of material care and neglect spiritual care. We should never be afraid to share our faith with them.

Once people develop AIDS, their families can care for them at home. Good ventilation and a clean environment are important to try to protect them from germs. Home should be the place

---

[117] "This is how we know what love is: Jesus Christ laid down his life for us. And we ought to lay down our lives for our brothers." (1 John 3:16) "Whoever claims to live in him must walk as Jesus did," (1 John 2:6) and surely Jesus showed compassion and care to the sick and suffering. "Anyone who claims to be in the light but hates his brother is still in the darkness." (1 John 2:9) "I was sick and you looked after me...whatever you did for one of the least of these brothers of mine, you did for me" (Matthew 25:36, 40).

where they receive the most love, and support. Hospital care may be needed when symptoms become severe.

Anyone coughing with untreated, active tuberculosis should be separated from others (see below). This is because of the tuberculosis and is true whether or not the person is infected with HIV. Apart from that precaution, *there is no need to segregate the person with AIDS from other family members*. Those close by cannot be infected with HIV from touching or from daily casual contact with the sick person. There is a small risk if the caretakers have open cuts or sores on their hands that come in direct contact with blood or sexual fluids from the person with AIDS. Even then the risk is small.

Volunteers from within the local church can support and help families to care for their loved ones. With simple home-based care kits, including gloves, bleach and perhaps some basic medicines, volunteers can make a valuable contribution to help the family. The volunteers can be encouraged in their work by giving them a small financial incentive, especially to cover their transport money.

People living with HIV/AIDS can also be involved in caring and visiting others who are also infected and needing care at home. The mutual support can be a great help to them.

If you are caring for the person with AIDS, you should wash your hands often with soap and water, especially after helping the person with his or her personal hygiene. You should also cover any wounds on your hands with a waterproof dressing. If possible, you should wear plastic or latex gloves, or polythene (plastic) bags when you clean up blood, diarrhoea, or any other body fluid that contains fresh blood. These measures are to protect you from any HIV entering through small cuts in your hands. You can buy gloves at a pharmacy for only a small cost.

Ordinary household bleach will kill HIV on the floors or bedclothes. Use one part bleach to nine parts of water. If you are using a bucket, mix one cup of bleach in a half bucket (nine cups) of water. Use a new solution of bleach every day. Also, check the date on the bottle to make sure that the bleach has not expired. The bleach should stay on the soiled area for 20 to 30 minutes.

It is important to keep the room, bed and skin of the person with AIDS as clean as possible. You should regularly sweep the floor (wash it if suitable), and wash the bedclothes. It is important to wash and dry the person's skin frequently. This is especially necessary if they are having diarrhoea. After washing, rubbing the skin with Vaseline can help keep the skin from breaking into sores. Clean but old wrappers (cloth or kangas) are useful as bedclothes, and a thick plastic cover for the mattress can help protect it.

> Frequent, small, tasty meals are often helpful...

Food and nutrition

Frequent, small, tasty meals are often helpful, rather than big, heavy meals once or twice a day. To keep the person living with AIDS as healthy as possible, these meals need to include body building foods (proteins) like beans, groundnuts, eggs, meat, fish or milk. They also should include starchy energy giving foods like maize, rice, yam, potato, cassava, and bread. Foods that protect the body from infection are also helpful. These are fruits and vegetables.

The body needs *vitamins,* special parts of food that keep the body working well. Because people with HIV often do not eat well, they should take multi-vitamins tablets or liquid. Multi-vitamins are safe, they are not costly, and they will help people remain with HIV remain healthy.

Mouth sores

Sometimes the person with AIDS develops a painful mouth. You can wash out the mouth with a solution of warm water and salt (just enough salt to taste like tears). Then use gentian violet (GV) solution to rinse the mouth. Make GV solution by mixing 2 teaspoons of full-strength GV in 2 cups of clean water. You can also paint the mouth sores several times daily with full-strength GV.

Diarrhoea

Diarrhoea is often one of the hardest symptoms of AIDS to deal with. Drinking plenty of pure boiled water helps prevent dehydration from the diarrhoea. If the diarrhoea is much and the person is becoming weak, you may need to give oral rehydration solution (also called oral drip, ORS, or ORT). Make this by mixing *two Coke bottles (30 cl each) of boiled water with one small level teaspoonful of salt and ten small level teaspoons of sugar.*[118] If boiling the water is not practical, use the cleanest water you can find. The person should drink at least half a cup of this along with some ordinary water or tea every time he passes diarrhoea. If someone is vomiting or does not want to drink this mixture, you may need to give them a large spoonful of it every few minutes until they regain their strength. In children up to two years of age, give half a small cup after each bout of diarrhoea. Over two years, give one cup, again with some ordinary water.

---

[118] Most countries have national or local guidelines for making oral rehydration solution, and you will want to follow the guidelines for your own area.

Bedsores

Lying in bed for long periods is not the best for people who are thin and sick because bedsores (ulcers) can develop easily. Help them to sit in a chair for some time every day, if possible, and to move around the room. To help prevent bedsores, rub with Vaseline the areas of the body where the bones are felt just underneath the skin (for example, on the hips). If someone cannot move from bed, turn them often in the bed so that the pressure of their body is not on one bony area for a long time. Prevention is extremely important because once the skin is broken and an ulcer develops, it is difficult to heal.

Pain control

Simple pain medicines such as aspirin and paracetamol (Panadol) can make someone with AIDS more comfortable. If they develop a high temperature, paracetamol can help lower it. Cool cloths on the body may also be soothing, but should not be used if they cause chilling. Antibiotics can treat many of the infections that cause pain and discomfort. Encourage the person to take all the drugs that the doctor or health worker has prescribed since they will likely help him or her feel better. If a certain medicine is too costly, ask the doctor whether a less costly one can be used in its place.

Cough and tuberculosis

Tuberculosis (TB) is common in Africa, Russia, Eastern Europe, most of Asia, and many other places. It is a serious illness and often fatal if left untreated. HIV-infected people often develop TB. Tuberculosis can cause different kinds of illness, but the kind that spreads easily to others is TB of the chest, which causes much coughing. Anyone who has been coughing for three weeks or more may have TB of the chest, especially if they are coughing up much phlegm. Coughing spreads the TB germs to others through tiny drops of fluid sprayed into the air. Anyone nearby can catch TB by breathing those tiny drops floating in the air. Small children and pregnant women are at greatest risk.

The best way to prevent TB from spreading to others is to encourage anyone with a chronic cough to be checked for TB and to take the full treatment if he or she does have TB. People are most likely to spread the illness before they begin treatment. Once they have had proper treatment for two to three weeks and are improving, they are unlikely to spread TB.

To reduce the spread of TB in droplets, encourage the person with TB to cough into disposable tissues, a container with a cover, or a cloth that can be stored in a polythene (plastic) bag. The cloth should be washed often.[119] Old newspaper or other waste paper can be used as tissues and then burned. The person with TB should be in a room with plenty of fresh air since moving air will help carry away the droplets.

It is important that people with TB take *all* their anti-TB drugs for as long as directed by the health worker. This will be for at least six months. Often, with good treatment, they can recover from TB and return to good health and strength. Proper treatment also helps prevent the TB from spreading to family and friends.

Children with AIDS

Most of what we said about caring for adults with AIDS is also true for children. Children need enough nutritious food (see recipe for pap on page 61). They need to be held and loved. They need hugs and kisses. They need you to treat them like

---

[119] *Hope at Home*, World Relief. Published in Nigeria by Africa Christian Textbooks, TCNN, Bukuru.

other children, to play with them and appreciate them. Their lives may be shorter than others' lives, but you can help make them special and blessed.

Children with HIV should receive all the usual childhood immunisations, except that a child with symptoms of AIDS should not be given BCG vaccination. The doctor or health worker will probably prescribe co-trimoxazole (Septrin or Bactrim) daily for children with AIDS or signs of weakened immune systems. This helps protect them from certain diseases. Health workers should also prescribe co-trimoxazole for babies of HIV-infected mothers from the age of four weeks to at least six months or a year, even when the babies appear healthy. This helps prevent *Pneumocystis carinii* pneumonia, which commonly affects HIV-infected infants.

Caring for the care-givers

Families and other daily care-givers can easily become exhausted by the constant demands of caring for those with AIDS. This gives the local church a wonderful opportunity to be involved in caring for the care-givers. Volunteers can go into the home regularly to allow the care-giver to shop, go to school, go to church, or just get a complete break. Pastors, elders, and church members can offer encouragement, prayer, counselling, and practical support.

Simple funerals

The number of burials (funerals) of people who have died from AIDS is daily increasing in all of our countries. Many already-poor families are using money they themselves need for food, housing, school fees and sometimes medicines. They spend large amounts of money on funerals, especially on lavishly decorated and expensive coffins, food, special burial cars, video taping of the service and other luxuries.

As Christians in our communities, we should lead the way in having simple, inexpensive, prayerful and dignified funeral services that show love and respect for the deceased and also show our faith in God. We do not believe God wants us to spend large amounts of money on burials. Expensive funerals do not help the people who have died, and they often cause great hardship to the family left behind.

If the family, especially the spouse or parents of the deceased, gives the pastor permission, he tan talk about HIV/AIDS at the funeral service. This can be an effective time to create awareness. The pastor should speak words that are as gentle and compassionate as they are truthful and challenging. Such open talk about HIV/AIDS will help others to speak openly about their sickness, may lead them to the help they need, and will reduce the stigma of HIV/AIDS in the community.

In conclusion, the love, support and care of family and friends can do much to help people living with HIV/AIDS live healthier, longer, more fulfilling and more productive lives. Remember, caring for someone with AIDS will not give you AIDS.

Discussion Questions

1. What cultural practices in your community are helpful in AIDS care or prevention? How can you encourage them?

2. If you know someone living with HIV/AIDS who is lonely and shunned by church members, discuss ways that you can change the situation.

3. Pretend that you are helping plan your own funeral. How would you plan it so that it would be consistent with what you believe and value? Would you want your family to spend much of their money for your funeral?

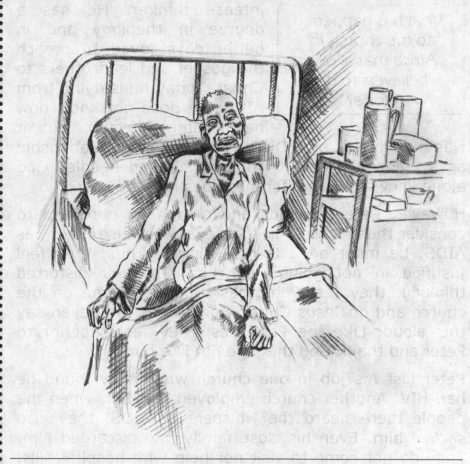

No one has come to sing

The hospital ward is stifling and confined. In the corner, the thin, dark outline of a man lies still on a bed, a piece of half eaten bread on his chest. His chest moves rapidly up and down as he gasps for air, creating a hustling sound. His mouth is parched, and breadcrumbs stick to his chapped lips. His skin is hot to touch.

This gaunt and almost unrecognisable figure is Peter, my treasured friend. He is a gentle young man, an

> What has happened to the church in Africa that allows believers to die alone?

intense thinker. He has a degree in theology and in better days loved to preach the gospel and lead others to Christ. Today he is dying from AIDS. He does not know how he became infected, but it was many years ago. Did he have a sexual relationship as a teenager? Was it from an infected needle? God alone knows. What difference does it make now?

However, Peter's friends and church do not want to consider these issues. In their eyes, because Peter has AIDS, he must be a terrible sinner. Thus, they feel justified in not going near him. In their distorted thinking, they feel Peter has brought shame on the church and on Jesus Christ. Sometimes they even say this aloud. Like the Pharisees, they feel superior to Peter and thank God they are not like him.

Peter lost his job in one church when they found he had HIV. Another church employed him but, when the people there heard the whispers of AIDS, they also sacked him. Even his close family has discarded him. They do not come to visit nor help with hospital bills. His uncle tells him he has brought disgrace on the family and has disappointed their expectations of him.

Today he lies in his hospital bed, his body weak and thin from the constant diarrhoea and fever. He grasps my hand and whispers, "There is no one here to sing." I bow closer to him to hear his barely audible words again, "No one has come to sing." This young man is dying alone. No one should have to die alone. *What has happened in Africa that allows people to die alone?*

What has happened to the church in Africa that allows believers to die alone?

I feel anger at AIDS, the robber of life, health, hope and reputation. I abhor the way it has destroyed Peter. I feel distress with him for how others have despised him. My heart breaks for him. I feel such sorrow that those who call themselves Christians do not understand the gospel of grace. Do they not know that none of us deserves God's mercy? Do they not know we are all sinners, whether we have AIDS or not? Do they not understand that all of us deserve hell? I want to tell them that only faith in the death of Christ can save any of us. How can they reject my friend even if he got AIDS from a sinful act? Are they any better than him? I know I am not. "God be merciful to me, a sinner."

My eyes sting with tears. With faltering words, I remind Peter of his Saviour, who also was despised and rejected by men, a man of sorrows and acquainted with grief. I assure Peter that Jesus took our sins and our sorrows on him when he died for us. I am comforted that Peter knows Jesus. There is nothing else I can offer him but Jesus. But what else does a dying man need?

If God is for us who can be against us?

I open my Bible and read to Peter from Romans 8, assuring him that nothing at all can separate him from the love of Christ. "If God is for us, who can be against us? He who did not spare his own Son, but gave him up for us all—how will he not also along with him, graciously give us all things? Who will bring any charge against those whom God has chosen? It is God who justifies. Who is he that condemns? Christ Jesus who died—more than that, who was raised to life—is at the right hand of God and is also interceding for us. Who shall separate us from the love of Christ? Shall trouble, or hardship or persecution or famine or nakedness or danger or sword? As it is written, 'For your sake we face death all day long, we are considered as sheep to be slaughtered.' No in all these things we are more than conquerors through him who loved us. For I am convinced (persuaded, absolutely sure) that neither death, nor life, neither angels nor demons, neither the present nor the future, not any powers, neither height nor depth, nor anything else in all creation (including AIDS) will be able to separate us from the love of God that is in Christ Jesus."

Peter's sad eyes look up at me again. "Please write those verses out for me so that I can read them again and again," he whispers.

I will do that. But I doubt if Peter will be here tomorrow to read them. He will be safe with Jesus in heaven, a place of no more pain. A place where he will be complete, perfect, and able to rejoice once again.

Peter's health improved again but he died four months after I wrote this account. His wife told me that he asked her every day to read aloud the above verses from Romans chapter 8. She did this daily until he died. He would often repeat the verses to himself. Over and over he would say to her, "See my dear wife, even this AIDS has not separated me from Jesus' love." Peter died with that assurance.[120]

---

[120] Based on my personal experience (Jean Garland).

Discussion Questions

1. The church leaders did not allow Peter to continue serving God in the church. Why do you think they acted as they did? How would you act if you were a church leader faced with a similar situation?

2. Can you think of other Scriptures apart from Romans 8 that would be helpful to a person dying with AIDS? Mark them in your Bible for future reference.

Chapter Sixteen
The Role of the Church in Caring
for Children Affected by HIV/AIDS

All over Africa, millions of children are being left as orphans when a mother or father dies from AIDS. By 2010, 25 million young people in Africa under 15 years of age will have lost one or both parents to AIDS. In Rwanda, in 2003, there were 63,000 child headed households. Twelve percent of all the children of

Africa are orphans, and in ten African countries more than one in five fourteen-year-olds is an orphan.[121] As a church and community, these children affected by AIDS are *our* children. We are responsible for them. We must defend their rights. African extended families have a strong tradition of caring for their orphans, and many uncles, aunts, and grandparents are doing all they can. The church must support and build on this strength. In many areas, though, the problem of children affected by HIV/AIDS is becoming so big that families trying to care for orphans are strained beyond what they can bear. God is calling his people to bring his church into this important work.

Children affected by HIV/AIDS are caught up in feelings and events that they do not understand and that threaten to destroy them. They face great emotional and psychological stress. Sometimes their grief may be overlooked as small and unimportant compared to the adults' grief. However, when a child loses a parent he or she feels great confusion and sorrow. When both parents are lost the shock is even worse.

Younger children do not understand that death is final—they wait for the parent to return. At the time of loss, they may continue to play as if nothing has happened, expressing their grief only later. Bereaved children have many developmental and emotional needs because of the trauma. In their grief, they may be angry, refuse to eat, or hurt other children. Sometimes they blame themselves and may need a caring adult to explain that they did nothing to cause the death.[122]

The church champions the rights of orphans

All too often, orphans are not well cared for. They may even be seriously exploited. Children orphaned as a result of HIV/AIDS

---

[121] *Africa's Orphaned Generations.* UNICEF. 2003.
[122] Ibid

suffer even more than many other orphans. In some parts of Africa, people may say these children are cursed because the parents had AIDS. This may mean these vulnerable children are not welcomed into the homes of those who could care for them. If the dead parents were never formally married in church, and perhaps no bride price was paid, then the extended family may feel little responsibility to help. Even families that do take in the orphans may treat them differently from their own children. For example, the orphans may receive less food, do more work, and be last to receive school fees.

Recently, someone told me of two small children whose parents had died from AIDS. Now they lived with relations, but the new family despised them because of their parents' illness. These children were not even infected with HIV, but the family did not allow them to eat with the others and expected them to do most of the work at home. This story is repeated again and again.

One young girl tells her story like this: "I waken early in the morning and do the sweeping and washing and cook breakfast while my aunt's children are still sleeping. I never get time to study and my aunt does not let me go to school. She beats me."

Another girl says, "I love to go to school because there I do not think about the problems at home. I awake at 4 am. Bathe the younger ones, sweep and cook, and then I walk four kilometers to school. We have to act like adults. We have to do what adults do and no one treats us like children any longer."

Another tells her story: "We are five staying with our uncle now. He is very old. Our father died in 2000 and our mother died last year. I am the oldest girl. I am thirteen. I am so scared of what will happen to us if we have to leave here. Where will we go? Will we be able to stay together? Will I have to care for my sister and brothers? Where will we get money and food? I don't want to be a prostitute."[123]

Orphans have a right to be heard and to be protected from abuse, neglect, maltreatment and exploitation. They also have the usual needs of children, including economic, social, educational, medical, emotional and spiritual needs. For example, they

> Defend the cause of the fatherless, plead the case of the widow.
> Isaiah 1:17

have a need (and a right) for their home and land—their own place. That is an important part of who they are. But what usually happens when a father dies, whether from AIDS or another cause? It is common all over Africa for an uncle or other male relative to come and take the land and the house, even if the mother is still alive.

The church must involve itself with these children. The local church with its spiritual authority and wisdom is often in the best position to be their champion, to defend their rights. If we do not defend them, who will? In the first chapter of Isaiah, God sets forth his accusation against his people. One of their great sins was worshiping false gods. Another was the failure to defend the widows and orphans. "Learn to do right! Seek justice, encourage the oppressed. Defend the cause of the fatherless, plead the case of the widow" (Isaiah 1:17).

Some children are taken advantage of, even sexually. Some have their land taken away from them because there is no one to stand up for them. The best way to protect the land is having the dying parent write a will. Caring adults and a loving church

---

[123] *Investing in Our Future, Psychosocial Support for Children Affected by HIV/AIDS* published by UNAIDS, July 2001.

community can make a huge difference in protecting the children's rights. They can know the laws in place to protect children and can watch for any physical or mental abuse.

Sexual exploitation is a serious risk for children, especially girls, orphaned or displaced because of HIV/AIDS. These girls are likely themselves to become infected. The church must reach out to protect them.

A love song in the Bible tells of a man and a woman preparing to marry. The writer speaks of a "sister" whose "breasts are not yet grown." He speaks of building a tower and a hedge or wall around this little girl. He speaks like an older brother who loves and protects her until she is ready for marriage (Song of Songs 8:8–9). The church can be the "older brother" to girls who become orphans. If a man tries to take advantage of a young girl, men and women in the church can place protection around her. When she is old enough for love and marriage, a family in the church can take the parent role in helping to make marriage arrangements.

Women in the church can be the orphan girl's special friend. They can form a group for all young girls to teach them basic skills of taking care of their bodies, understanding the changes in their bodies as they mature, knowing how to tell men "no" to sex before marriage, and how to marry the right man. They can learn about cooking and farming and raising children. These are skills that girls usually learn from their mothers but that orphaned girls can learn through the church.[124]

---

[124] Some ideas taken from taken from *Our Children: The Church Cares for Children Affected by AIDS.* World Relief Corporation, 2003.

The church supports the extended family

All over Africa children are caring for dying parents with AIDS. Many households are headed by children caring for their younger siblings. It is not easy for children to head a home. They need guidance to help them make wise choices in life. A family headed by a child needs another caring family walking alongside.[125] Caring Christian adults can make a great difference in the lives of these children. God loves them more than we ever can, with an unending love.

Likewise, all over Africa grandparents are left to care for children affected and infected by HIV/AIDS. In villages in east, central and southern Africa, we find grandparents who are caring for up to twenty-five orphan grandchildren. The elderly grandparents need the help and support of the church family to ease their load.

How can the church help? One way is by financial assistance to extended families that lack the means to care for the orphans. The money can pay for food, soap, medical care, school books and school fees. Good schooling and a caring family will help the children grow into responsible adults. The church may also need to be an advocate for the children to help them find a school or a family to care for them. The church can help older children to care for their younger brothers and sisters. The African proverb, "It takes a village to raise a child," is true.[126]

What else can local congregations do to support the extended family? Can someone in the family or church foster the children (take care of them as their own for a time)? Is adoption a possibility, especially for tiny babies the family is unable to care

---

[125] *Our Children: The Church Cares for Children Affected by AIDS.* World Relief Corporation, 2003.
[126] Ideas taken from Debbie Dortzbach of World Relief, which has developed strategies for orphan care.

for? The role of deacons in the church is caring for people in need. They can mobilise church members to plant and cultivate the farm, repair a home, take someone to the hospital, visit the sick person, and act as parents for children affected by AIDS. Some churches have special ministries to grandparents to help them care for their grandchildren. If older children can be sponsored to receive an education, they can go on to help care for the younger family members.

Being part of the church means that we care for each other. "Greater love has no one than this, that he lay down his life for his friends." (John 15:13) The local church must use its energies and talents to care for children affected by HIV/AIDS. The body of Christ should care for its own. The Apostle James tells us, "religion that God our Father accepts as pure and faultless is this: to look after orphans and widows in their distress and to keep oneself unspotted from the world" (James 1:27).

Orphans and soon-to-be orphans may lack opportunity to attend school. Some African churches have turned their benches during the week to create schools for orphans and children who cannot attend school because they are at home caring for their dying parents. Church members volunteer as teachers. Youth group members and teachers from the church can tutor these children at home in the evenings. It is important to work and play with these young people in a purposeful, planned way *before* they become orphans. This means pastors need to be preaching on the topic regularly to prepare congregations to accept some of the responsibility for children at risk in their communities.

A church in Malawi worked together to farm a bit of land. They sold the food from the land and used the money to care for AIDS orphans in the church. Other churches give struggling families small "micro-enterprise" loans to help them begin supporting themselves again. Some women's fellowship groups collect grain each week to distribute to widows, orphans and the families caring for orphans. Here is an idea from the Evangelical Churches of West Africa Women's Fellowship. As each woman prepares daily meals, she takes just one handful of dry grain from what she will cook and stores it in a bucket. As the month goes by, the grain in the bucket mounts up. At the monthly women's fellowship meeting, the small amount of grain from each woman's bucket is collected, with singing and dancing, into sacks. Then, the women distribute the grain to needy families in the community. A little from each family, when added together, becomes enough to make a big difference to those in need.[127] The Scriptures teach us that as the family of God we need to share our food. God says, "Is this not the kind of fasting I have chosen: is it not to share your food with the hungry and to provide the poor wanderer with shelter—when you see the naked to clothe them, and not to turn away from your own flesh and blood?" (Isaiah 58:6–7).

Carry each other's burdens

We encourage churches to help care for children affected by HIV/AIDS, but we are not rejecting the responsibility of the extended family. The church's goal is to *support* the extended family and help them carry the extra load, "and in this way you will fulfil the law of Christ" (Galatians 6:2).

The time of crisis when a parent dies is not the best time to settle the question of how the children will be cared for. The pastor or the family head should bring together family members to decide what to do with the children when the parents die.

---

[127] Seeds of Love project of The ECWA AIDS Ministry, Jos, Nigeria.

Ideally, this happens while the parents are still living, but sometimes it may have to be after they die. This kind of discussion gives everyone the chance to share the responsibility. One family can take the child into the home, another may help with money for food and school fees, while another may agree to provide clothing.

The African church must make a long-term commitment to care for children affected and infected by HIV/AIDS. The church is in the best position to respond to the crisis: not only is there a church on most of the street corners in Africa, but also, God has *commanded* the church to serve (Acts 4:33–35). He has given us gifts of service and positions in the church such as deacons and deaconesses (Acts 6:1–7). Let us *use* those gifts and resources to God's glory by ministering effectively to those in need.

Orphanages and alternatives

God placed children in families for good reasons. It is much better for orphans to remain in their own communities near their homes than to move far away to orphanages. The extended family should care for them whenever possible, supported by the local church, school and friends in the familiar community. In some places, however, where AIDS has reached devastating heights, the number of orphans is simply too great to be absorbed by the extended family and the church. In these areas orphanages of some kind are needed. In some communities, only children are left to work on the farms and to walk the streets.

Many have seen serious difficulties with the traditional orphanage, where large numbers of youths live far from the influence of elders and families. However, the huge masses of children cannot wait, and we cannot leave them abandoned. This has required people to open many orphanages throughout Africa, even though this solution is far from the best. We have heard it said that building large orphanages is "an expensive way to increase our problem." Still, a well-run, caring orphanage is a better solution than leaving children trying to survive on the streets.

As an alternative to traditional orphanages, Rev. Angelo D'Agostino of Kenya has suggested a model for the future: "Cities of Hope" where children would live with the elderly in 300–400 acre plots, living and learning together and growing crops for their sustenance.[128] This type of community-based orphan care could be one of the better solutions. It would help with the important task of keeping children in touch with their extended family as much as possible. It would involve men as well as women in orphan care. Boys and girls need positive role models of godly men in their lives. Too often, orphan care is left to women alone.

The church and community also must be involved in caring for HIV positive orphans, who will need special help to live as full and joyful lives as possible, in the knowledge of God's love for them. As ARVs become more available for children with HIV, they will live longer. These precious children should be cared for with the same compassion and dignity as those who are not HIV positive. They are innocent sufferers of an extremely unkind disease and must not be left out of any orphan care programme.

Preparing children for loss

Some ministries have become quite experienced in helping these children and preparing them for their parents' deaths. Talking to children about death in advance gives them time to get used to the idea and gradually loosen the bonds of

---

[128] Prescription for Hope conference, Washington DC, February 2002.
http://www.aegis.com/news/pr/2002/PR020344.html

attachment.[129] Children who have the opportunity to say good-bye and to hear last words of advice greatly appreciate that occasion after the parent is gone.

Children can experience much healing when they have the chance to say actual, thought-out good-byes to people, places or a familiar family group. Parents, children and others can exchange wishes and blessings. This helps prevent the children from blaming themselves and leaves less unfinished business to complicate the grief process. Pastors and church counsellors may be the best ones to help with this process of saying good-bye.

The memory book

A *memory book* is a journal of facts and memories for children who are facing the loss of a parent. This idea started in Uganda and is now being used in many countries in Africa.

When children are separated from their parents, their memories and identities tend to fade. The memory book seeks to keep memories alive and to strengthen the child's sense of belonging. It is also a way for a parent to introduce their children to the fact that he or she has HIV and what that means. The parent or parents write information and personal stories into the book. The different headings or titles can be such things as:

- My favourite memories of you
- Your health
- Information about your father and mother
- Family traditions and special events
- The family tree

---

[129] *Investing in our future: Psychosocial support for children affected by HIV/AIDS: UNAIDS best practice collection,* UNAIDS, July 2001.

- Family photographs

The child may help write in the book while the mother or father is still alive. It is a tool to help the parent and child to deal with the past, present and future.

Children are often moved to a different location when they are orphaned. The memory book helps remind them of their roots so they do not lose their sense of belonging. It reminds them of where and from what people they came. It also helps parents understand their child's fears about the future and helps them decide where the child will live after the parent's death. The book should even be helpful in preventing AIDS, because the children witness and understand the ordeal the parent is going through and do not want to repeat it.

Will the church meet the challenge?

The church in some parts of Africa is already facing the orphan crisis on a large scale. Elsewhere the number of orphans is just beginning to grow. As the AIDS epidemic continues, we will *all* be forced to deal with the crisis. If we do not, we will be failing an entire generation and will have thousands of street children in our cities leading to more crime, violence, prostitution, and the general decay of our continent.

Congregations and church governing councils need to explore the issue and start deciding now how to help families. We need to welcome creative thinking about solutions. Maybe women's and men's fellowships could find ways to help families who are struggling to care for orphans. Can we set up houses near the church where we, the church and community, can help raise orphans in a secure environment? Can church members tithe their household's food monthly to help feed orphans?

Most likely the answers will not come from the government or large organisations. Rather *you* the reader will be the one to move into action in your own community and church. You are the one who has begun to understand the problem, and you are the one who is in touch with your own congregation and community. Do not wait for someone else to find the answer, for by then it will be too late. Instead, work with those around you, begin talking with others in your church, discover what needs already exist, and begin to *act*.

Our desire is that every local church will soon respond to the AIDS orphan crisis with the love of Christ. These young people are not to blame for the deaths of their parents, and they need us to care for them. If we do not, many of them will be lost as well and may drift into behaviour that causes them to die from AIDS just as their parents did. The cycle of suffering will continue.

Discussion Questions

1. Are local churches already caring for orphans in your community? How? Are there still unmet needs?

2. How do you think the local church *should* be or *could* be caring for orphans in your community?

3. What are some models of orphan care that your community could put into practice as the number of AIDS orphans grows? Which model seems best to you? Why?

4. Do you see any problems with children growing up in an orphanage where the involvement of their extended family and community is not possible? Discuss.

Hard to Believe: A Story from Zimbabwe

**By Eugenia Imagine Ndlovu,
Age 16, Zimbabwe**

Usually the truth is hard to believe.
It takes a century to believe the truth,
But the lies are really easy to believe,
They take only a fraction of a second to believe.
I really don't know why the situation is like this.
When she told me,
I thought I was dreaming.
I thought there was something wrong with my ears.
I could not ask questions because I thought it was a story
    about someone.
Or just something that happened years ago to someone else.

It was hard to believe.
It was as tough as counting all the stars in the sky.
It was hard to believe because it was a true story.
I had to believe because it was true and real.
It was a very long story filled with sorrowful words.
It was filled with very painful words, which stay in your heart
    forever.
It's a story to remember because it was the most painful and
    saddest story for me in my life.
It's a story you would hear while crying tears of blood,
But I did not cry because it was a shock to me and too hard to
    believe.

After listening, you would pray to the Lord to take you out of
    this wicked world the next hour.

All because this is and shall be the most painful story to you
   and me.

It's a story that happened to someone I'm really close to.
Someone so special to me at good and bad times,
Someone with a long lasting love for me.
She is always by my side.
She is the queen of my heart.
She cares and love me.
She loves me, and I love her too.

I know you wish to know who she is.
It's hard to believe that something very bad like that can
   happen to someone who you never wanted to feel any
   pain.
It's also hard for me to say who she is but I have to say it
   because you need to know.
It's.......my......mother.

It is good to know that your parent or relative is HIV
positive. It is even better if your parent tells you on his
or her own rather than your asking after seeing a book
or hearing it from other people. It's just as painful to
find out on your own. AIDS is not something to hide;
it's something natural. It is a disease like any other life
threatening disease. Parents who are infected by
HIV/AIDS and children who are affected need support,
but most importantly, they need love.

I discovered my mother's status by error. I saw a tape
that had my name and my brother's name written on
it. I listened to it, only to discover that the voice on
the tape was my mother's and she was talking to us. I
was shattered when she said she had HIV and my first
reaction was that she was going to die. Then she

explained to me that the tape was three years old and I started to believe that there was hope of her survival for a long time. Then she explained everything to me about HIV/AIDS. I believe she told me of her HIV status because she loves us and she loves others by positively living with HIV/AIDS.

I get support from her immediate family, especially from her sister who is like a mum to me. Her friends are also a good source of support and so are other HIV/AIDS activists who are infected and affected. Some people talk of my mum as being very courageous but others point fingers at me or talk in low voices or in corners. I just brave it and say that they are the ones with the problem and not me because I know HIV can happen to anybody at any time.

As a person who has a mother living positively with HIV, I would like to thank all the children who have gone through thick and thin in supporting and taking care of their ailing parents. There is life after being HIV positive and we continue to live after our beloved ones are gone. To those who have parents who are infected, I leave you with this special message: never give up on life, pray for those infected and affected, but don't forget to pray for yourselves. As my mother says, "HIV for me means Hope Is Vital."[130]

---

[130] *Investing in Our Future, Psychosocial Support for Children Affected by HIV/AIDS,* UNAIDS, July 2001.

Discussion Questions

1. Discuss the statement that Eugenia makes, "It is good to know that your parent or relative is HIV positive. It is even better if your parent tells you on his or her own rather than your asking after seeing a book or hearing it from other people." Is she right?

2. What difference does it make to all involved when a mother or father tells the children of their HIV status?

3. After reading Eugenia's story, why do you think she is so positive about living with HIV in her family?

Chapter Seventeen
AIDS and the Church

The Christian Church in Africa is in a uniquely key position to address most of the aspects of the HIV/AIDS pandemic. It has extensive reach and its influence filters through most African communities. The church has a massive, yet often untapped, potential to successfully reverse the course of the pandemic. Its core values of love, care, support and justice have produced the nurturing and development of strong Church-run care and support programmes in many communities. At the same time, its promotion of abstinence before marriage and faithfulness in marriage, which can be strengthened, is an essential weapon to reduce HIV/AIDS prevalence and incidence in Africa. But sadly stigmatization and discrimination still abound within the church, and seriously slow down, and sometimes reverse progress towards preventing and controlling HIV/AIDS.[131]

Having the mind of Christ: attitudes of the church towards HIV/AIDS

Sadly, the world often sees the church of Jesus Christ as a place where sinners are not welcome. They say the church is only for

---

[131] Pan African Christian AIDS Network Symposium on HIV/AIDS, Nairobi, 2003.

"good people." We wrongly think or even say, "Bad people are not welcome in our church." And in our minds, we see those with HIV/AIDS as the worst of the bad!

Since the arrival of the AIDS epidemic, there are few secret sins with such obvious outward results. Therefore, the church often thinks it can comfortably reject those suffering with AIDS. "They are only getting *what they deserve* as a punishment for their sin" is the spoken or unspoken judgment. We think we see a direct cause and effect, and we have it all arranged neatly in our minds.

Getting what we deserve?

What would happen if we *all* received what we deserve for our sin? *We would all go to hell.* Not one of us deserves heaven. God sees our heart and thoughts, and every one of us at times thinks sexual, lustful thoughts. Jesus said that those who lust are equally guilty of the sin of adultery (Matthew 5:27–28). In addition, what about those who do commit adultery or fornication and do not get AIDS? Are they less guilty? What of those who sin by cheating, being ungrateful, hating a brother, or envying the world's riches? Are they less guilty?

God is a *holy* God and cannot even look on sin. He is a *just* God and always punishes sin. If we think we are good and righteous, we fail to see that in God's sight we are all sinners, and every one of us deserves hell fire. If we are on our way to heaven, it is only because God in his mercy and love has chosen us to be his own. Our only hope is that he has brought us to faith in Jesus Christ as our Saviour, and that all of our sins have been paid for when God punished Jesus for those very sins. He was our sacrificial lamb when he became the atonement for our sins (Isaiah 53).

Do we truly understand grace? Do we think something good in us is what saves us? We deserve death and hell as much as any other person, with or without AIDS.

> If we claim to be without sin, we deceive ourselves and the truth is not in us.
>
> If we confess our sins, he is faithful and just and will forgive us our sins and purify us from all unrighteousness.
>
> If we claim we have not sinned, we make him out to be a liar and his word has no place in our lives.
>
> My dear children, I write this to you so that you will not sin. But if anybody does sin, we have one who speaks to the Father in our defence—Jesus Christ, the Righteous One.
>
> He is the atoning sacrifice for our sins, and not only for ours but also for the sins of the whole world.
>
> 1 John 1:8–2:2 (NIV)

With a true understanding of grace as our foundation, we can serve God in the area of HIV/AIDS. We can show infected people unconditional love, knowing we are no better than they. We can teach others not to point the finger. We can come to God for our own forgiveness, and then go out to give that forgiveness to others in the name of Jesus Christ.

The example of Jesus

"It is not the healthy who need a doctor, but the sick. I have not come to call the righteous, but sinners" (Mark 2:17).

We are often too concerned with the question of *punishment* for sin. That was not the emphasis of Jesus. When we hear of someone suffering with AIDS we want to think or even voice the question, "Do they have AIDS because of adultery or fornication? Are they guilty? Is the spouse guilty? Is that why they are suffering?" This focus helps us relieve our own conscience and feel better in our self-righteousness.

Jesus and his disciples came upon a man who was blind from birth (John 9). The disciples just *knew* this must be a punishment for someone's sin. The only detail they wondered about was *whose* sin. They asked, "Who sinned, this man or his parents?" The disciples wanted the same answer as we so often do: whom to blame. Jesus' answer refocused their attention from the issue of blame to the glory of God: "Neither this man nor his parents sinned, but this happened so that the work of God might be displayed in his life."

Another time some people brought Jesus news that Pilate had cruelly killed some Galilean pilgrims. The crowd thought the victims somehow deserved their fate—maybe they were wicked. Jesus firmly corrected their error: "Do you think that these Galileans were worse sinners than all the other Galileans because they suffered this way? I tell you, no! But unless you repent, you too will all perish. Or those eighteen who died when the tower in Siloam fell on them. Do you think they were more guilty than all the others living in Jerusalem? I tell you, no! But unless you repent you will all perish" (Luke 13:1–5).

All creation is experiencing judgement for sin. That is why there is pain and sickness in our world. Some suffering has a clear cause and a direct effect. Often that is true for AIDS. However, not all those with HIV/AIDS lived immoral lives. Some are victims of someone else's immoral life or of an accident such as a needle prick or transfusion. They are suffering as part of the judgement of sin since creation, and not for a specific sin. And as Jesus' words remind us, even those who became infected because of sin are not necessarily greater sinners than all the rest of us. The results of their sin may simply be more visible, but no less deadly, than the end result we all face.

While Jesus sat at the well, a woman came all alone to draw water. As he talked with her, Jesus knew she was an unbeliever, of a different religion, and had lived a life of adultery. Yet he showed interest in her, answered her questions, offered her living water, and even drank from her cup. So he gave her hope. As a result, she believed in him and led many of her friends to come and meet the Messiah (John 4).

The church leaders brought the frightened woman to Jesus and forced her to stand before him while they brought the condemnation: "Teacher, this woman was caught in the act of adultery. In the Law Moses commanded us to stone such women. Now what do you say?" Jesus was silent, but the leaders kept questioning him. They knew he had compassion and was a "friend of sinners," but what could he say about one who was such a terrible sinner, bringing shame on herself?

"When they kept on questioning him, he straightened up and said to them, 'If any one of you is without sin, let him be the first to throw a stone at her.' Again he stooped down and wrote on the ground. At this, those who heard began to go away one at a time, the older ones first, until only Jesus was left, with the woman still standing there. Jesus straightened up and asked her, 'Woman, where are they? Has no one condemned you?'

'No one, sir,' she said.

'Then neither do I condemn you,' Jesus declared. 'Go now and leave your life of sin'" (John 8).

Jesus did not approve of the woman's sin. He did not hide it, deny it, or ignore it. He called her to *repentance:* "leave your life of sin." However, he also refused to condemn her. What is more, he reminded the accusers that they too were guilty of sin. What about us? Are we ready to throw the stone? Or will we, with Jesus, draw the sinner to repentance and forgiveness?

Jesus went through all the towns and villages, teaching in their synagogues, preaching the good news of the kingdom and healing every disease and sickness. When he saw the crowds, he had compassion on them, because they were harassed and helpless, like sheep without a shepherd. Then he said to his disciples, "The harvest is plentiful but the workers are few. Ask the Lord of the harvest, therefore, to send out workers into his harvest field" (Matthew 9:35–36).

Compassion is what Jesus felt when he saw the crowds of lost people, oppressed by sin and evil. His reaction was not to condemn but to heal, deliver, and forgive. Not only that, but he was so moved with the need that he told his disciples to pray for even more workers to bring in the harvest of forgiven, redeemed sinners. Jesus had compassion for the sick, no matter the origin of their sickness. He is our example.

The way we care for those with AIDS should be a radical picture of Christian love following the example of Jesus Christ our Saviour. If we truly understand who we are, sinners forgiven and bought by the blood of Christ, we will not stumble in our determination to care for those with AIDS.

Jesus the Servant

Your attitude should be the same as that of Christ Jesus:
Who, being in very nature God, did not consider equality
with God something to be grasped,
but made himself nothing, taking the very nature of a
servant, being made in human likeness.
And being found in appearance as a man, he humbled
himself and became obedient to death—even
death on a cross!

Philippians 2:5–8

Do you remember the story when Jesus took the place of a servant and washed his disciples' feet? "Jesus knew that the Father had put all things under his power, and that he had come from God and was returning to God, so he got up from the meal, took off his outer clothing….and began to wash the disciples' feet" (John 13:3–5).

We need to understand that Jesus knew who he was—God's Son and indeed God himself (verse 3). He also knew his place in God's plan, that he was to die for the whole world (verse 1). Still, he was able to humble himself to be a servant and wash the disciples' feet. He did this to show that true love is humble, sacrificial service, just as he himself was to lay down his very life for the world.

Likewise, when we know our true position in God's world, sinners only made God's children by faith in Jesus Christ, he makes us able to be servants. We serve others who need to see and feel the love of Jesus Christ. "Now that I, your Lord and Teacher, have washed your feet, you also should wash one another's feet. I have set you an example that you should do as I have done for you" (John 13:14–15).

Romans 15:1–2 urges us to "Bear with the failing of the weak and not to please ourselves. Each of us should please his neighbour for his good, to build him up." This reminds us that we are to seek to serve and encourage even those whose faith is weak, who may seem less spiritual than we think we are.

Cautions against judging others

The Bible teaches clearly that our desire towards the sinner should be to draw him or her towards forgiveness in Christ. While we are to recognise sin, warn sinners and even exercise discipline for unrepentant sinners in the church, we are never to pass a sentence of judgment and condemnation—only God can do that. Our warnings and our discipline are for the purpose of drawing the sinner into the body of Christ, not for excluding him or her.

The church can do much to change people's attitudes towards those living with HIV/AIDS. This will lessen the stigma of the disease. Jesus said, "Do not judge, or you too will be judged, and with the measure you use, it will be measured to you" (Matthew 7:1–2).[132] James 2:12–13 says, "Speak and act as those who are going to be judged by the law that gives freedom, because judgment without mercy will be shown to anyone who has not been merciful. Mercy triumphs over judgment."

Romans 2:1 tells us that we have no excuse for condemning others when we ourselves are sinners: "You pass judgment on someone else, for at whatever point you judge the other, you are condemning yourself, because you who pass judgment do the same things."

Recognising this, the Pan African Christian AIDS Network declared, "As the Church of Christ we should condemn stigma and discrimination in no uncertain terms. We resolve to call on the church to be a place of refuge, grace and unconditional love instead of judgment and rejection."[133]

Does compassion mean we are excusing sin?

Sometimes we fear that if the church shows compassion to those with HIV/AIDS, people will think we are overlooking sexual sin. That is not what we are saying. God commands us all to repent of sexual sin. When people with or without HIV/AIDS continue in sexual sin, they are not following God's

---

[132] Also "Do not condemn, or you will be condemned. Forgive and you will be forgiven" (Luke 6:37).

[133] Pan African Christian AIDS Network Symposium on HIV/AIDS, Nairobi Kenya, 2003.

path. The church needs to exercise church discipline in those situations. God commands all of us to *turn* from our sins and *return* to obedience. However, God also commands us to show compassion to those who are suffering and to accept the repentant sinner into fellowship with the rest of us repentant sinners (Psalm 103:4, 8, 13–14; Luke 17:3; Galatians 6:1).

Paul told the churches in Galatia how to deal with a sinning member. "Brothers, if someone is caught in a sin, you who are spiritual should restore him gently. Carry each other's burdens, and in this way you will fulfil the law of Christ" (Galatians 6:1–2). Notice the balance: the spiritual members of the church are to restore the sinner, but to do so *gently,* out of love. Compassion is an expression of love and is part of the fruit of the Spirit (Galatians 5:22). To lack compassion and love for those who are suffering goes against the teaching of Scripture and is a serious sin itself.

Paul's teaching is quite helpful in showing us the relationship between discipline and restoration:

> If anyone has caused grief, he has not so much grieved me as he has grieved all of you, to some extent—not to put it too severely. The punishment inflicted on him by the majority is sufficient for him. Now instead, you ought to forgive and comfort him, so that he will not be overwhelmed by excessive sorrow. I urge you, therefore, to reaffirm your love for him. The reason I wrote you was to see if you would stand the test and be obedient in everything. If you forgive anyone, I also forgive him. And what I have forgiven—if there was anything to forgive—I have forgiven in the sight of Christ for your sake, in order that Satan might not outwit us. For we are not unaware of his schemes (2 Corinthians 2:5–11, NIV).

There are several important points here.

- The sinner was a church member who had sinned and was unrepentant. Therefore he was placed under church discipline.
- He has now *responded* to the discipline with repentance.
- The sinner has been *forgiven*—by Christ and by Paul, and the church also is to forgive him. Paul instructs the church "to forgive and comfort him," not to continue rejecting him or sending him away.

The reasons Paul gives for forgiving, comforting, and drawing the person back into fellowship are "so that he will not be overwhelmed by excessive sorrow" and "in order that Satan might not outwit us." Paul is saying that this repentant brother is at risk of being crushed by sorrow and discouragement. If that happens, it is not a victory for the church, but rather playing right into the hands of Satan himself. Satan would love to see the brother cast aside to drift alone in despair, rather than knowing forgiveness and getting back into the spiritual battle again.

I was sick and you looked after me.

Jesus said that if we help and care for those who are hungry, thirsty, sick, naked, homeless, or in prison, then we are actually caring for him (Matthew 25:31–46). On the other hand, he condemns those who do not show this kind of love: "I was hungry and you gave me nothing to eat, I was thirsty and you gave me nothing to drink, I was a stranger and you did not invite me in, I needed clothes and you did not clothe me, I was sick and in prison and you did not look after me." Which will Jesus say to you, "I was sick and you looked after me," or "you did *not* look after me?"[134]

The role of the church in preventing AIDS

So far, we have discussed the call and opportunity for the church to care for those affected with HIV. The church also has much to do in the role of *prevention,* and is in a powerful position to change the future of AIDS in Africa. Will we save or abandon the generations of orphans? Will millions with HIV/AIDS see God's love and mercy or the coldness of false religion? In countries where AIDS is only now becoming obvious, will we stop the epidemic or follow the tragic course of many other African countries? The answers depend on how the church responds right now before it is too late. Will we act to help quench the fire before it has burned the whole house?

Some denominations have already set up their own AIDS awareness programmes to educate pastors, church leaders, women's fellowship groups and young people about AIDS. But how many of our theological colleges have courses about HIV/AIDS on their training curriculum for pastors and theological students? Every one of our institutions needs good training opportunities for its students to learn how to teach others about AIDS and how to mobilise congregations to respond to HIV/AIDS in their midst. This includes dealing with such issues as orphan and vulnerable children, stigma and discrimination of those infected, home-based care, and preparing for death. The best curriculum that I am aware of

---

[134] Help with this section from "Choosing Hope, The Christian Response to HIV/AIDS." *Curriculum for Theological Colleges,* MAP, Kenya. Printed in Nigeria by Africa Christian Textbooks, TCNN, Bukuru.

originated in Kenya and is called, "Choosing Hope. The Christian Response to HIV/AIDS."[135]

It is my prayer that, over the next decade, the number of Christian AIDS ministries in Africa will multiply one thousand fold. I recently had the privilege of hearing the Uganda's First Lady Mrs Janet Museveni speak about AIDS in Uganda. In that country, all sectors of society have been aggressively fighting HIV since 1986. Eighteen years later, the number of new cases of HIV infection is falling. Uganda is the only country in Africa where this is clearly the case. But Mrs Museveni told us that in Uganda, with a population of only 22 million people, there are more than 2000 organisations fighting AIDS. It has taken the combined effort of 2000 organisations more than eighteen years to turn the tide of AIDS deaths there.

Mrs Museveni pointed out that the church in Uganda has been one of the most effective bodies in fighting AIDS. She said programmes emphasising sexual abstinence until marriage have changed behaviour. Many young Ugandans are now making wise decisions about sexual behaviour, and deaths from AIDS are falling.[136] If the church of Jesus Christ in all Africa can do its part, we can turn the tide of death in the whole continent. I pray it does not take us eighteen years to do so, or many more millions will be lost to AIDS. Many will die without Christ and without hope, and there will be untold suffering for all concerned.

---

[135] "Choosing Hope, The Christian Response to HIV/AIDS." *Curriculum for Theological Colleges,* MAP, Kenya. Printed in Nigeria by Africa Christian Textbooks, TCNN, Bukuru.

[136] Mrs Janet Museveni, Prescription for Hope conference, Washington DC, 2002.

What the church must teach about sex

Sometimes it seems the message of sexual abstinence before marriage and faithfulness inside marriage is the "vaccine" that few people want. Sexual activity before and outside of marriage, however, is the main reason that AIDS is spreading so quickly. It is certain that if there were no promiscuity there would be no epidemic of AIDS. About 90 percent of those living with HIV/AIDS contracted the disease by sexual intercourse with an infected person. If the church is to play a role in preventing AIDS, it must be actively involved in teaching the Biblical view of the place of sex in the family and society. The age-old phrase "prevention is better than cure" has never been more relevant.

However, the church needs to not only teach about adultery and fornication from the pulpit, but also to teach young people the life skills needed to live pure lives. The church should be helping them to deal with the pressures that society today is placing on them.

My work with Scripture Union and Fellowship of Christian Students "life-skills programme" has shown me that information about HIV alone cannot change behaviour in a lasting way. Rather we must teach young people to respect themselves as unique and special. We must show them that they are made in God's image, that God has a unique purpose for their lives, and that his rules are best for them. These concepts are powerful tools for helping them to make good decisions in the area of sex as well as in the rest of life. The Scripture Union and Fellowship of Christian Students materials "Adventure Unlimited" for junior secondary schools and "Choose Freedom" for senior secondary schools and tertiary institutions are useful materials for communicating the vital messages to young people.[137] Likewise, the "True Love Waits" materials developed in Malawi include a complete curriculum for teaching life-skills to young people. In Nigeria, we have developed one curriculum for training secondary school Christian religious knowledge teachers and another for Islamic studies teachers. These courses for teachers equip them to teach their classes about AIDS not only with accurate scientific information, but also with a solid moral viewpoint. Part of this curriculum is how to teach young people life-skills for dealing with sexual temptations and pressures.[138]

The words of one girl living in crowded university lodgings are ringing in my ears. "I'm fed up listening to one more talk about AIDS," she said. "You tell us how many people are dying and how we get AIDS, but no one is helping us to stop getting it! We need help to know how to have the strength to stop having sex when everyone around us is sleeping around. If you don't do it, you are weird. You have no idea how hard that is!"

Peer teaching

A powerful way for the church to communicate God's plan for life and relationships to young people is to use youths themselves to teach each other. Peer education is important. Maybe the local church could give youth fellowship leaders the opportunities they need to be trained in life-skills education, then allow them to teach life-skills to their peers. A slogan we heard often at the 2003 International Conference on AIDS and Sexually Transmitted Diseases in Africa (ICASA) was, "There is nothing for us without us. We want to part of the solution,

---

[137] "Choose Freedom" and "Adventure Unlimited" are available in French and English from Scripture Union offices and staff in many African countries

[138] Faith-Based AIDS Awareness Programme, IICS, University of Jos, Plateau State, Nigeria.

and not the problem." In other words, youth want to *participate* in finding and carrying out solutions.

Our youths have many talents and abilities ready to use and develop. Athletics is one. Sporting activities organised by church youth are a great way to reach out and share God's plan with other young people. In the same way, many youths are talented in drama, music, writing, art, and other communication skills. Encourage them use their talents to pass this life-saving message. Find ways to fit their abilities into the church's programmes.

There is a wonderful future for the young people of Africa if only we can keep them alive!

Sexual purity is essential for the Christian

Christians in leadership positions in the church can begin teaching by *example* how to avoid AIDS. The most important way to do this is by living sincere, admirable Christian lives themselves. Sadly, too many marriages of Christian workers do *not* shine forth the message that they are enjoying marriage in the way that God has planned. In a moral climate where casual sex is joked about and accepted as normal, the voice of the church guided by God's Word needs to speak strong and clear. The church needs to proclaim the message clearly: God *does* know what is best for our happiness, and his plan is for no sex before marriage or outside of marriage, and great sex within marriage.

It is easy for us to slip into agreeing with the way the world around us is thinking. As we watch television programmes and listen to the words of many popular songs, it becomes almost automatic to accept that sex before and outside marriage is unavoidable and even acceptable. We see advertisement boards that use sex to promote products and we laugh at the idea. One current advertisement declares "Your wife is having an affair with…." It ends with the brand name of a washing machine and cooker! Another urges wives to "keep their men at home" by using a certain brand of cooking oil!

Rather than following the thinking of the world, we are called to be *different!* "Do not conform any longer to the pattern of this world, but be transformed by the renewing of your mind" (Romans 5:12). If we are to obey God's commands, we must be willing to live differently from the world as well as from our traditions and follow God's pattern for holy living. We must replace the world's thoughts and ideas with those from God's Word.

The Christian's body belongs to Christ and is to be a pure temple for the Holy Spirit (1 Corinthians 6:15, 19–20). Jesus purchased the believer with his own blood. Sexual impurity violates the holiness of that temple and is a sin against the person's own body (1 Corinthians 6:18). Marriage is the only place for sexual relations that are pure and holy (Hebrews 13:4). Christians must keep pure in their sexual behaviour. Failure to do so is a grave sin against their own bodies and takes away from God's glory in their lives.

The Bible is clear that some people have a special calling from God to lead a single (unmarried) life. And, of course, many of us spend a significant part of our adult lives as single, before marriage and after the loss of a spouse. Single people are more free to use all of their energies to serve the Lord. The unmarried person should abstain from sexual relations (1 Corinthians 6:9–7:8, Ephesians 5:3), and thus will not be at risk from AIDS.

Marriage is given as a provision for the one who cannot remain single and also pure (1 Corinthians 7:2, 9) and is also God's provision for demonstrating his love, giving us children, and establishing families.

celebrate sex!

In the church's witness to the world regarding HIV/AIDS, we must make clear that God calls us to celebrate sex as his gift. Christians should not be against sex, only against its misuse. In God's wonderful plan of marriage, sexual satisfaction and pleasure are not only allowed but *encouraged*. (1 Corinthians 7:3–5). God's original intention was for one man to be married to one woman (Matthew 19:5, 1 Corinthians 7:2). Within the marriage, each spouse is responsible for meeting the sexual needs of the other. It is wrong for either husband or wife to refuse to meet those needs.

When husband and wife are meeting their mate's needs, neither will be easily tempted into sexual sin outside of the marriage (1 Corinthians 7:4–5).[139] The only exception is that both husband and wife may *agree* to abstain from sexual relations in marriage for a *limited time* of prayer (1 Corinthians 5:7). Married couples who are faithful to each other are not at risk from AIDS, unless one of them brought HIV into the marriage at the beginning.

The Bible also teaches that marriage is to be a life-long commitment (1 Corinthians 7:10–12). A separated or divorced husband or wife is easily tempted into sexual sin,

---

[139] See footnote 94 on page 152 for this passage in the New Living Translation.

possibly leading to HIV infection.[140] Divorce is a violation of the "one man, one woman" principle of marriage, and is equivalent to adultery in that it destroys the union that God has blessed (Matthew 19:9).

Living according to God's standard is the best way to avoid AIDS, to glorify God, and to enjoy his plan for our lives.

The role of the church in advocacy and best practice

The church, that is you and I, must be involved in making our voice heard on behalf of those living with HIV/AIDS and on the issues surrounding HIV/AIDS. We need to speak up when policies are being made or programmes are being developed in relation to people living with AIDS. This is true at the local church level, but also at the national and international levels. Poverty and Third World debt greatly affect those living with HIV/AIDS, and so Christians need to be at the forefront of efforts to deal with such issues.

AIDS ministry should be done with the highest possible standards for the sake of people and to give glory to God. We need monitoring and evaluation methods to judge what is the "best practice" in any AIDS ministry. We, the church, must be as professional as possible in all that we do, including writing reports and documenting our work. Sadly, church organisations are often slow to document the good work we are doing, and therefore we are the last to get the financial help from donor agencies that can help us to do our work.

---

[140] *Choosing Hope. The Christian Response to HIV/AIDS.* MAP, Kenya.

Other ways that the church can encourage its members to be more involved in the AIDS issue

- World AIDS Day (always December 1st). Why not use this day to teach about HIV/AIDS? Why not have special prayer for those suffering, and awareness meetings in all areas of the congregation's life? You can distribute red ribbons for members to wear, with the aim of helping them be more willing to talk about AIDS with their neighbours. There are many visual aids, especially videos, that you can use effectively in gatherings. Panel discussions and question and answer sessions would be helpful. You can find people living with HIV/AIDS who are walking with the Lord to speak to these gatherings. This would be an encouragement to them, and often a strong warning to others.
- Valentine's Day, sometimes known as Lover's Day, is February 14. Why not use the day as an opportunity to teach the Bible's perspective on love in marriage? Or, you could use the day for married couples to renew their wedding vows to each other.
- Why not use Sunday services to teach about AIDS and give God's perspective on the issue?
- Why not train church volunteers for home-based care? They could be of great value for people living with HIV/AIDS in the church and community.
- Use posters about AIDS displayed in the church building to educate the congregation.
- Help the church become the chief advocate for the rights of those living with HIV/AIDS, making sure that they are not stigmatised or discriminated against.
- Let the church encourage families to adopt and foster children orphaned by AIDS.

- Encourage the women's fellowship groups to collect grains for widows and orphans. This is just one way they can begin caring for those in the community who are affected by AIDS (see page 266 for details)? [141]

The church's responsibility to pray

This book opens with the words of 2 Chronicles 7:14, a promise that encourages us to pray.

"If my people, who are called by my name, will humble themselves and pray and seek my face and turn from their wicked ways, then will I hear from heaven and will forgive their sin and will heal their land."

Surely, one of the most important things that Christians can do is pray for God's intervention in the AIDS crisis. We need to pray for a great miracle in our nations. God is able to change hearts and situations by his almighty power.

- Pray that the people of our nations will humble themselves before God and seek his face as we try to stop the epidemic.
- Pray that God, by his Holy Spirit, will lead people to repentance from their immoral behaviour.
- Pray that marriages will be strong and husbands and wives faithful to one another.
- Pray that those already infected will have courage to live with their disease and come to repentance and faith in Jesus Christ, with a sure hope of heaven.
- Pray that God will bring comfort, strength, patience and endurance to those who are suffering and facing death.

---

[141] Some of these ideas taken from Paul B. D. Mershak. *The Response of the Church to the HIV/AIDS Epidemic.* seminar paper, Fellowship of Christian Students, 2001.

Pray that he will help them overcome their fears and have peace in their hearts.

- Pray that God will help the orphans and the widows and show us how we can help them.
- Pray that the church of Jesus Christ, his hands and feet here on earth, will do what Jesus would do in caring for those with HIV/AIDS.
- Pray that scientists will find a cure for AIDS and a vaccine to prevent it.
- Pray that antiretroviral drugs will become more available for people who need them.
- Pray for pastors and church leaders to have the wisdom to teach about AIDS and lead their people in ministry to those who need it.
- Pray for greater public awareness and that our governments will do more to fight HIV/AIDS.
- Pray for those who are secretly living with HIV/AIDS and have no one to trust for help. Pray they will find friends and ultimately find God as their comfort.
- Pray for those who are lonely and bereaved because of AIDS, that they will be comforted and strengthened to meet the days ahead and trust and hope in God's goodness and mercy.
- Pray that in all we do, God will receive glory, especially as the non-Christian world sees believers caring for others in the midst of suffering and death.

Discussion Questions

1. Do you think the statements and teachings of church leaders influence sexual behaviour? Do they reduce the spread of AIDS, have no effect at all or maybe even increase the spread of AIDS?

2. Should Christians work with non-Christian groups in fighting AIDS in the community? What can Christians offer that non-Christians cannot offer? Would their approaches be any different?

Trading with God

I sit quietly and absorb the atmosphere created in a room filled to capacity with friends greeting and chatting with one another. This November afternoon, I am at an HIV/AIDS Support Club. But this is no ordinary meeting of people living with HIV/AIDS. There is no sense of hopelessness or despair here. There is laughter and joy. I look at the faces. Some are extremely thin. The faces of three young women are severely scarred by the herpes infection that often comes with HIV. One has already lost sight in one eye and has a cosmetic replacement that clearly improves her appearance. They noisily exchange news and greetings with their friends.

"Good to see you again. How is your family? How are the children? How is the sickness?" They are talking and embracing their sisters and brothers, delighted to be here again with their equals, fighting together in the struggle to live optimistically with HIV. Some are extremely thin, but several are still strong and healthy looking with clear skin and bright eyes. No one would guess the common enemy, HIV, is hiding in their bodies.

As I look around the gathering, I notice there are more women present than men. I learned later that most of the women are widows whose husbands have already died from AIDS. Men are often slower to come for support, but some men are here today, too. All the participants are young and some are single, but all have a common bond with their friends at the club. HIV has come to stay with them all.

But what is the secret of their strength and joy, when all of them are facing sorrow, shame, sickness, pain and premature death?

The group leader asks how many have been involved in trading. Most of the women raise their hands. She says, "When you trade, you give something away in return for something better." They all understand the concept. The leader continues, "We are going to sing our theme song again today, which tells us we can trade with God. And as we trade, our loving Father gives us something much better in return."

With heart-felt fervour they all start to sing the following words.

"I'm trading my sorrows, I'm trading my shame, I'm laying them down for the joy of the Lord."

"I'm trading my sickness, I'm trading my pain, I'm laying them down for the joy of the Lord."

Their voices become stronger as they sing and almost shout the chorus to the song,

"Yes Lord, Yes Lord, YES, YES Lord, Amen."

As they sing, all of the participants raise their hands, punching the air, creating together a defining moment as they affirm the truth of the words they are singing.

As I watch their radiant faces, my eyes fill with tears because I know miracles are happening in this room. These dear men and women all know the agonising sorrow AIDS is bringing to their families. They know the burdening shame they feel at their illness. They know the constant sicknesses they are enduring. They know real pain in their bodies, and often worse, the hurt of rejection by those close to them. They have come together today united in one experience: when they come to the Lord Jesus, laying their sorrow, shame, sickness and pain at his feet, he gives them his pardon, peace and joy. These dear friends know the joy of the Lord is their strength.

One young woman beside me stands shyly before the group. She tells them with quiet voice and a smile, "For a long time I have been bitter about how my husband brought me AIDS. But now, I am no longer bitter because God has helped me to forgive my husband. And now I am trusting Jesus to forgive my sin too." The group rejoiced with her.

Another attractive young lady tells how she recently asked a pastor to pray for her, and how God has been giving her renewed physical strength. Others stand confidently and tell of answers to prayer in their lives.

A young man tells me he had planned to marry, but with the testing required before the wedding he found he had HIV infection. Now he says he wants to use his experience to talk to many young people about how to avoid AIDS. He says, "I want God to use what is happening to me as a warning to others."

One woman has her two young children with her. Both of them also have HIV and show its signs on their skin. Their mother tells me her husband died from AIDS five years ago and her oldest son, now in secondary school, is the only one in the family without AIDS. "It is not easy for us. It is only God who helps me. I am often lonely. But it is only God who gives me strength. I am trying to roof a small house for my son so he will have somewhere to live when we all go."

Later, I talk to another widow. She married her husband five years before. He died two years ago. One child has already died from AIDS. The other, a little boy of two, needs to be tested again to see if he is infected. Once again, I hear the testimony, "God is helping me."

As the afternoon progresses, we eat together, talk about diet, medicines and exercise, and have fun together in a "treasure hunt" as we search for little treats hidden around the building. The place reverberates with squeals and laughter. Later, we spend time praying for each other's needs. We make plans to go next month for a picnic outside the city. Everyone agrees that the picnic is something to look forward to eagerly. The encouragement of being together means so much to these dear ones. Today one woman even paid a week's wages in transport money to attend the club.

Many of us are expert traders, and as AIDS is bringing untold suffering and death, the product of the enemy, these friends of mine are learning to *trade with God.* They are surrendering to him their sorrows, shame, sickness and pain. In return, He is giving them an abundance of his joy and peace. I see this as an exchange that passes human understanding and gives abundant hope. Where there is Christ there is hope, and where there is hope there is life.

Conclusion

AIDS is Real and It's in Our Church. But there is hope—hope found in God's Word. Hope for those who are not infected, if they follow God's pattern for life, but also hope for those who are infected as the church responds with compassion and ministers in Jesus' name. As one group of African Christian leaders declared:

> Remember we are people of faith who believe in the power of the Holy Spirit to bring about positive life change. This not only provides a foundation for prevention, but it also impels us to provide care, support, hope and love. When all is said and done, our drive to care, prevent, and advocate must be Christ centred. The truths which call us to look to Christ are:
>
> - the example all encompassing He set by His life
> - the love infinite He demonstrated by His death
> - the power without limit demonstrated by His life after death
> - the hope now and eternal for those who trust in Him.[142]

---

[142] Pan African Christian AIDS Network Symposium, Nairobi, 2003.

We conclude this book with a quote from the Kampala Declaration of 1994:

> The Church is God's instrument to proclaim and promote life. AIDS is the opposite of life. We believe that God has called us at this unique moment in history to be instruments of his hope and eternal life. His life and hope may yet be seen even when sickness consumes our bodies and a virus saps the strength of those we love.
>
> We plead for God's people to engage in dialogue at all social and structural levels and wrestle with the issues, so that we might understand and apply principles of truth in a way that will bring about appropriate change which must include some traditional cultural practices as well as some modern trends that affect the family.
>
> We are watchmen standing in the gap and stewards of the hope of God offered in Christ. The pain and alienation of AIDS compels us to show and offer the fullness and wholeness that is found in him alone. In this, our time of weakness, may the rule of Christ's love bring healing to the nations.[143]

Amen.

---

[143] *AIDS in Africa, the Church's Opportunity.* MAP International, 1996.

What Christians Believe

Perhaps, though you are reading this book to learn about HIV/AIDS, you are not sure what Christians believe. Or perhaps you have come from a family that has been Christian for many generations and you are used to the ideas of Christianity. No matter what your situation, we hope that you will take time to read this summary of what Christians believe. It is important to know about HIV/AIDS, but it is much more important to know God and know how to live in his power and love.

Here is a short explanation of what Christians believe. These things are told in the Bible. The Bible is a collection of writings written by many prophets and people of God over many generations. God inspired, or directed, the writers, giving them the words that he wanted to reveal to people everywhere. Taken as a whole, the Bible is the story of the way God loves people and how he is saving them from the powers of evil and death. Here, then, is the story.

There is only one God. He is all powerful, all merciful, all knowing, and completely just and fair in all he does. He created everything there is. He created the earth, sun, moon, stars, life, plants and animals, light, energy, and people. God is completely good, true and pure, without any trace of evil or lie. Therefore, when he had made the whole world and everything in it, he looked at it all and saw that it was very good. He was pleased with the world, which was full of beauty and peace.

God also created spirit beings called angels to worship him, serve him, and do his will. One powerful angel, Satan, rebelled against God and set himself up as God's enemy. God threw Satan out of heaven along with other angels who had joined Satan as enemies of God.

God made people different from the animals. He breathed his own spirit into them, making them in some ways like him. He made both man and woman "in his own image," giving part of his glory, beauty, and value to them both. He made them able to think, love, speak, enjoy beauty, tell stories, make good things, and have children. He made them to rule in his name over the world he had created. God created people because of love, and he took great joy and delight in the love they had for each other and for him. Likewise, the first man and woman, named Adam and Eve, were happy and content and enjoyed being with God and being loved by him.

One day, though, Satan came to Eve in the form of a snake and tempted her to disobey God. She listened to Satan and disobeyed God, and so did Adam. By their actions, they brought evil and destruction into the world. Rebelling against God, doing what is wrong, is what we call "sin." All people since Adam and Eve have sinned against God. God is perfectly good and cannotapprove of sin or overlook it. He punishes all evil.

The beautiful world God had created began to suffer. Death, hatred, suffering, fear, and sickness entered the world. This is why we now have suffering and illnesses such as HIV/AIDS and many others. People were cut off from God. Instead of worshiping the true God, they began to make their own gods and worship them. The more people turned away from God, the more they forgot who he was. God sent messengers called prophets to tell people he loved them and they should turn back to him. The people did not listen. They went even farther from God and did all kinds of evil things. There seemed to be no hope. It appeared people would never return to God, and would be lost forever. (You can read about this in the *Old Testament* section of the Bible.)

God still loved people and had a plan to save them from their evil ways and from the power of Satan. He did an amazing thing. He came into this world himself by becoming a man. This man, who was also the one and only God, was named Jesus. He lived on earth about two-thousand years ago. He taught people to turn from their sin and return to God. He said that he had come to set people free from every kind of evil and slavery. He did many miracles such as healing the sick, making blind people see, and even raising some people from death. He drove powerful evil spirits out of people just by speaking a word. These miracles showed the mighty power of God and the way it overcomes evil. They show us today that God is stronger than every kind of evil and disease including HIV/AIDS.

Jesus taught people how to live as God wants them to live. He said they should show each other love and faithfulness. He said they should live pure, honest, good lives. He said they should not trust in money or power. He said people who trusted and believed in him would be forgiven and would live forever. He said that he had come to give his life to save us from our sins and make us children of God if we would only believe in him and follow him. You can read about the life and teachings of Jesus in the New Testament in the Bible.

Many people, especially the religious and government leaders, did not like Jesus' message. They killed him by nailing him to a wooden cross. How could he be killed, when he was so good, holy, and powerful? The answer is that he willingly *gave up his life* so that he could take the punishment of our sins. Our sins had separated us from God, and death was the punishment. God loved us so much that he willingly suffered that death for us to make us free from sin and death.

There is more good news. Jesus had told his followers that he would be killed and would rise from the dead, although they did not understand his meaning. But, as he had told them, he did come alive again three days after he died. Over several weeks, he came to his followers several times and explained to them how he had died to set us free from sin and to give us life that never ends. Many people saw him alive. After that, he said he must return to heaven where he came from. He breathed his Spirit on his chosen followers and told them to go and tell everyone the good news, and to tell everyone that they should hear and obey what Jesus had said. Then, while his followers watched, he rose up into the sky and disappeared. Jesus promised that he will return to the earth again and that the whole world will know then that he is King of Kings and Lord of Lords.

Here, then, is the good news of Jesus:

- God loves us very much, no matter who we are or what kind of person we are. He loves us whether we are men, women, or children. He loves us whether we are young or old, European, African, Asian, or from elsewhere. He loves us whether we are farmers, soldiers, traders or the president. He loves us even though we all have sins, uncleanness, and weaknesses.

- God is pure and just. He always punishes evil. But, because of his love, he himself took the punishment for our sins in the death of Jesus.

- Jesus showed us God's amazing power. He showed that he is King over the world, nature, and every kind of spirit. His miracles and rising from the dead showed that he conquers illness, pain, hatred, death, sin, and Satan himself.

- We do not have to live and die cut off from God. We do not have to live in fear of evil, witchcraft, illness, and death. We can be saved from all that. We must simply turn away from our sins, make God our master and put our trust in him to save us through what he did for us in the death and rising again of Jesus.

- When we turn from our sins and trust God to forgive us through Jesus, he makes us completely clean from all our sins. He puts us under the protection of his mighty power. In fact, he changes us from the very centre of our being, making us his children, part of his family.

- At the same time, God removes from us the curse of death, and gives us life that never ends. He assures us that even though our bodies die, we have unending life and happiness. Not even death can separate us from God. Jesus said, "I am the resurrection and the life. He who believes in me will live, even though he dies; and whoever lives and believes in me will never die."[144] He promises that just as he rose from the dead, so shall we.

- God does all of this as a free gift. It is not because of anything we have done, because we can never be good enough by our own efforts. Christians call this free gift and goodness of God "grace."

You can read more about Jesus and his message in the Bible. The first four sections or "books" of the New Testament are called the Gospels of Matthew, Mark, Luke, and John. Each one

---

[144] John 11:25–26

is an account of Jesus' life, teaching, death, and rising. Jesus said that people who truly search for God will find him. He said that the words he spoke were words of life. Whether or not you are already a follower of Jesus, we challenge you to listen to all that Jesus said, and to ask God to show more and more of the truth as you hear and obey his words of life.

Resources

Alliance, A. *Building Blocks: Africa-Wide Briefing Notes*, 2002. http://www.aidsalliance.org.

Barnett, T. and A. Whiteside. *AIDS in the Twenty-First Century: Disease and Globalization*. Palgrave Macmillan, 2002.

Bayley, A. *One New Humanity. The Challenge of AIDS*. SPCK, Cambridge, 1996.

Baylor International Pediatric AIDS Initiative. *HIV Curriculum for the Health Professional*, 2003. http://bayloraids.org/africa/

Brand, P. Leprosy and AIDS. *Pain: The Gift Nobody Wants*. P. Yancey and P. Brand. Harper and Collins, 1993.

Brown, R. and T. Macharia. *HIV/AIDS Case Studies*. Christians Concerned about AIDS in Kenya (CCAK), Nairobi, 2004.

Cunningham, D. The Window of Hope. *Towards an AIDS-Free Generation*. Scripture Union. Ghana, 1997.

Derbyshire, M. *Friends in Need: A Handbook for the Care of Orphans in the Community*. Viva Network, 2002. www.viva.org/-tellme/resources/articles/fin.pdf

Dixon, P. *AIDS and You. Revised Edition*. Eastbourne, Kingsway, 1991.

Dixon, P. *The Truth About AIDS*. Eastbourne: Kingsway Publications, 1994. http://www.globalchange.com/ttaa/

Dortzbach, K. and N. K. (editors). *Helpers for a Healing Community, a Pastoral Counselling Manual for AIDS*. MAP International, Nairobi, Kenya, 1996.

FAO. *Living Well with HIV/AIDS: A Manual on Nutritional Care and Support for People Living with HIV/AIDS*, 2002. http://www.-fao.org/DOCREP/005/Y4168E/Y4168E00.HTM

Fountain, D. AIDS: The 15/45 Window. *Evangelical Missions Quarterly* 34(1), 1998. http://bgc.gospelcom.net/emis/1998/aids.htm

Fountain, D. *Teaching Our Children God's Ways*. MAP International, 1999.

Kilbourn, P. *Children Affected by HIV/AIDS: Compassionate Care*. MARC: World Vision Publications, 2002.

MAP. *Choosing Hope. The Christian Response to the HIV/AIDS Epidemic. Curriculum Modules for Theological and Pastoral Training Institutions*. MAP International, Nairobi, 1999.

McDowell, J. *Why Wait?* Here's Life Publishers, 1987.

McGeary, J. Death Stalks a Continent. *Time*, 2001.

McSweeney, L. *AIDS—Your Responsibility*. Ambassador Publications, Ibadan, 1991.

McSweeney, L. *A Challenge to Love: Changing Behaviour*. Ambassador Publications, Ibadan, 1995.

Ministry, T. E. A. *AIDS Seminar Handbook. All About AIDS*. The ECWA AIDS Ministry (TEAM), Jos, Nigeria, 2001.

Muraah, W. M. and W. N. Kiarie. *HIV and AIDS: Facts That Could Change Your Life*. English Press Ltd, Nairobi, 2001.

Prescription for Hope. *Ministry, Informational and Preventative Manual for Those Dealing with HIV/AIDS*, 2001.

Saunderson, P. TB and AIDS in the 1990s. *Footsteps* 19, 1994. http://footsteps.tearfund.net/english/pdf/19e.pdf

Shorter, A. and E. Onyancha. *The Church and AIDS in Africa: A Case Study*. Paulines Publications Africa, Nairobi, 1998.

Stine, G. J. *AIDS Update 2003*. Prentice Hall, New Jersey, 2003.

TEAM (The ECWA AIDS Ministry). *Caring for People with AIDS. Home Based Care*. TEAM, Jos, Nigeria, 2001.

UNAIDS. *AIDS Epidemic Update 2003*. UNAIDS, Geneva, 2003.

UNAIDS. *Investing in Our Future: Psychosocial Support for Children Affected by HIV/AIDS. A Case Study in Zimbabwe and the United Republic of Tanzania*. UNAIDS, 2001. http://www.unaids.org

UNAIDS. *Report on the Global HIV/AIDS Epidemic*. UNAIDS, Geneva, 2001.

UNICEF. *HIV and Infant Feeding*. UNICEF, 2002. http://www.unicef.org/publications/index_5387.html

WHO. *Living with AIDS in the Community*. Global Programme on HIV/AIDS, Geneva, 1992.

Wood, G. G. and J. E. Dietrich. *The AIDS Epidemic: Balancing Compassion and Justice*. Multnomah Press, Portland, Oregon, 1990.

World Relief. *Blessing. The Story of Rwandan Churches Challenging the AIDS Crisis*. World Relief Corporation, Rwanda.

World Relief. *Hope at Home. Caring for Family with AIDS*. Published in Rwanda by World Relief. Published with permission in Nigeria by ACTS, TCNN, 2003.

World Relief. *Our Children: The Church Cares for Children Affected by AIDS*. Published in Kenya by World Relief, HIV/AIDS Programmes, 2003. Published with permission in Nigeria by ACTS, TCNN, 2004.

Web Sites

If you have access to the Internet, there are many resources available to you—articles, news, pamphlets, and even entire books. We are giving *only a few* examples here but you will find many others. Note that we do not necessarily agree with all the information on any of these sites. Each one is operated by a different organisation with its own viewpoint and policies. Some sites have resources in languages other than English, and most of the sites have links to help you explore further.

AEGIS (AIDS Education Global Information System)
http://www.aegis.com
News, facts, resources. Oriented more towards developed countries, but has much useful information for everyone.

AIDSInfo (USA National Institutes of Health)
http://aidsinfo.nih.gov

AIDS Education and Training Centers (ATEC)
http://www.aids-etc.org

AIDS Map
http://www.aidsmap.com/
Links, resources for developed and developing countries.

Christian Connections for International Health
http://www.ccih.org
Many resources on HIV/AIDS and other topics of health and development.

Family Health International (FHI)
http://www.fhi.org

HIV InSite
http://hivinsite.ucsf.edu
Many useful and up-to-date resources and links. There is a separate section for issues relevant to Africa. The Knowledge Base is a comprehensive textbook on all aspects of HIV/AIDS. There is also page titled "Community-Based Care in the Developing World: Related Resources" with many links to other resources. Use the search box to find that page within the site.

International AIDS Alliance

http://www.aidsalliance.org
Includes resources and toolkits useful in African countries, such as a toolkit for NGOs (non-governmental organisations) and those working with NGOs.

Reproline (Johns Hopkins University)

http://www.reproline.jhu.edu/
Includes PowerPoint and multimedia tutorials on care of women with HIV.

Synergy

http://www.synergyaids.com
Technical and programme development resources.

UNAIDS

http://www.unaids.org. Many resources and reports are available at this site, as well as latest news about international efforts against HIV/AIDS.

UNICEF

http://www.unicef.org/publications

Viva Network

http://www.viva.org
Networking and resources on-line in the area of caring for orphans and vulnerable children. Includes Chris-Caba electronic journal, focusing "on the special needs of Christians and Christian organisations working with children affected by HIV/AIDS."

Addresses

Africa Christian Textbooks (ACTS)

Copies of this book and others on AIDS, as well as theological books, are available from the following ACTS branches:

ACTS Headquarters:

Theological College of Northern Nigeria (TCNN)
PMB 2020, Bukuru 930008
Plateau State, Nigeria
Tel. +234-(0)73-281055, -281546, mobile +234-(0)803 5895328
Email: acts@hisen.org; web http://www.africachristiantextbooks.com

Other ACTS offices:

West Africa Theological Seminary (WATS)
No.35/37 Airport Road, Junction Bus Stop
Ajawo Estate, Ikeja
Lagos, Nigeria
Tel. mobile +234-(0)802-3670628

Samuel Bill Theological College (SBTC)
PMB 1060, Abak
Akwa Ibom State, Nigeria
Tel. mobile +234-(0)802-3471024

Nigeria Baptist Theological Seminary (NBTS)
PMB 4008, Ogbomoso
Oyo State, Nigeria
Tel. mobile +234-(0)803 3843152

Nairobi Evangelical Graduate School of Theology (NEGST)
Karen, Nairobi
Tel. Nbi 782362 or 0733 473311 or 0735 450156.

MAP International
PO Box 21663,
Nairobi, Kenya
Tel: +254-2-569513

Scripture Union International

Has national offices in many African countries. For contact information for your country, go to http://www.su-international.org or email enquiries@su-international.org.

Teaching-aids at Low Cost (TALC)
PO Box 49
St Albans
Hertfordshire AL1 5TX, UK
Telephone: +44 (0) 1727 853869
E-mail: talc@talcuk.org
http://www.talcuk.org

Index